Y0-BCR-602

Colossal Hamilton of Texas

A J Hamilton

Texas.

Colossal Hamilton of Texas

A BIOGRAPHY OF
ANDREW JACKSON HAMILTON

Militant Unionist and Reconstruction Governor

BY

JOHN L. WALLER

TEXAS WESTERN PRESS

THE UNIVERSITY OF TEXAS AT EL PASO

1 9 6 8

Edited by

S. D. MYRES

Designed by

CARL HERTZOG

Library of Congress Catalog Card No. 68-30890

[*vi*]

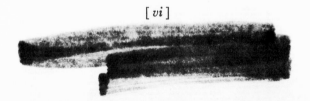

To

*Professor Charles William Ramsdell and
Professor Eugene Campbell Barker who
granted me a teaching fellowship which
opened the door of the Graduate School
of the University of Texas and a richer
and fuller life for me.*

PREFACE

THE LONG PERIOD *of violent political controversy preceding the Civil War, the prolonged, bloody fighting, with enormous casualties, and the embittered years of reconstruction and readjustment caused such deep-seated disturbances that even after a full century this period of history attracts the attention and energies of students and writers.*

Much new material on Texas history has become available during the present century. The publications of the Texas State Historical Association, theses and dissertations in local history, extensive newspaper collections, and new archival material—all throw a flood of light on the Civil War and Reconstruction. It is now quite evident that there was no unanimity of sentiment in the South for breaking the ties with the United States.

Andrew Jackson Hamilton, usually known and referred to as A. J. or "Colossal Jack" was the most articulate, eloquent, and aggressive of those in Texas who opposed secession. He was Military Governor of the State, 1862-1865, and was the first Provisional Governor during Reconstruction. He is the central character in this study. The militancy, often bitterness, of "Yellow Dog" Democracy has tended to consign Texas Unionists to oblivion. It is to be hoped that this book will in a measure restore Hamilton to his rightful place in the history of Texas.

The archives of The University of Texas at Austin contain many rich collections on the colorful history of Texas before, during, and after the Civil War. The following is a list of the materials that have proved most fruitful for the present study: William Pitt Ballinger, Diary, and Correspondence; Guy M. Bryan Papers; Ben H. Epperson Collection; Andrew Jackson Hamilton Papers; William Wallace Mills Collection; James P. Newcomb Collection; Oran Milo Roberts Correspondence and Papers; Ashbel Smith Collection; and

James Webb Throckmorton Correspondence and Papers. Mr. John H. Chiles, great-grandson of A. J. Hamilton, and grand nephew of W. W. Mills, recently transferred the Mills Papers to the archives of The University of Texas. The writer feels an indebtedness to Mr. and Mrs. Chiles for permitting him to use this material before it was placed in the archives, also for making available several pictures included in the book. Another valuable collection, the R. Niles Graham—Elisha Marshall Pease Collection, was recently acquired by the Austin Public Library. Mrs. James P. ("Miss Catherine") Hart, curator, was kind in giving me the opportunity to use the correspondence while it was being edited and shelved.

It was the good fortune of the writer to have access to the National Archives, where he received every courtesy from Archivist T. R. Shellenburger and his capable assistants E. O. Parker and Peter Condos. It should also be mentioned that Peter A. Brannon, Director of Archives and History of the State of Alabama, gave valuable assistance.

The Archives of The University of Texas contain a large number of M.A. theses relating to the local history of the State. The writer has profited from an association with Dr. R. L. Biesele, who, for many years supervised the M.A. thesis work in history, and who thus deserves special credit for assistance freely given. Miss Winnie Allen, archivist, and Mr. J. Evetts Haley were successful in acquiring valuable collections for the Archives. Dorman B. Winfrey, archivist for a short time, was energetic and efficient in organizing and cataloguing the materials, and thus making them available to students. Chester V. Kielman, his successor, has continued this work.

Dr. Winfrey served as State Archivist when its valuable records were housed in quonset huts on property of the Texas Highway Department. The writer did much of the research at this time and he is appreciative of the kindness and efficient help of Dr. Winfrey and his assistant, Mrs. Fletcher Osburn.

Joe Park, while in charge of the University newspaper library, was also most helpful. Dr. Llerena Friend, curator of the Eugene Campbell Barker Center of Texas History, not only made available its rich resources of Texas history, but also was generous in counsel and encouragement. Dr. Robert C. Cotner has given constructive criticism of much of the manuscript, and in addition has listened patiently to innumerable comments by the writer.

Dr. S. D. Myres, Editor Texas Western Press, has greatly exceeded the generally accepted requirements of the editor on a manuscript. He made two trips to Austin for long and constructive conferences. I am deeply indebted to him.

Dr. C. L. Sonnichsen, former colleague at Texas Western College (now The University of Texas at El Paso), offered constructive suggestions as the study and writing proceeded. Mr. J. J. Bowden, former student, has given much time to the manuscript.

Dr. Carl Hertzog, former colleague and Director of the Texas Western Press, pleased me immeasurably when he accepted the manuscript for publication. Dr. James M. Day helped with the proofreading and prepared the Index.

My thanks are also due the following for supplying the pictures that appear in this study: Mr. and Mrs. John H. Chiles of Austin, the Austin Public Library, the Library of Congress, and the National Archives.

My wife has been patient and sympathetic during the delightful time of research, and the painful period of organization and composition. For every word and act of encouragement I am sincerely grateful, but of necessity must accept responsibility for the account that follows.

JOHN L. WALLER

Austin, Texas
June 1, 1968

CHAPTERS

PHOTOGRAPHS
following page 68

Andrew Jackson Hamilton

Governor's Mansion

President Abraham Lincoln

Salmon P. Chase

Edmund J. Davis

Morgan C. Hamilton

Mary Jane (Bowen) Hamilton

Mrs. Hamilton and Jersey Cow

Fair Oaks—Hamilton Home

Hamilton's Pool

Elisha Marshall Pease

Alexander Watkins Terrell

Oran Milo Roberts

Svante Magnus Swenson

James Webb Throckmorton

George W. Paschall

Texas State Capitol

The Funeral Cortege

Colossal Hamilton of Texas

CHAPTER I

Young Alabamian in Texas Politics

LATE IN 1846 a relatively unknown young lawyer arrived in Texas from his native State of Alabama. Surprisingly, within less than a decade, this man—Andrew Jackson Hamilton— would become a political force to reckon with—and in a few more years he would virtually control, at least for a time, the government of the Lone Star State.

Once in Texas, Hamilton settled on a farm near La Grange in Fayette County, certainly an unlikely place from which to launch a political career. He brought with him his young wife and their two children, Mary and Frank; also two slaves presumably a gift from Mrs. Hamilton's father, a well-to-do plantation owner back in Alabama.

Born January 28, 1815, in Madison County, Alabama, (Mississippi Territory),[1] Hamilton was now only thirty-two years of age, but he was fully mature, both mentally and physically. He was a man of distinguished appearance: six feet tall; broad shoulders; an attractive face marked by a prominent nose, a wide forehead, and luminous blue eyes. His head was large, its top covered with a full growth of thick black hair.[2]

In addition, Hamilton was endowed with a strong and mellifluous voice, plus an unhesitating command of a rich, descriptive vocabulary. It was inevitable during the Golden Age of American oratory that a man so equipped would exercise

1. *United States Congress Biographical Dictionary of the American Congress, 1774-1961. The Continental Congress, September 5, 1774, to October 21, 1788, and the Congress of the United States, From the First to the Eighty-sixth Congress, March 4, 1789, to January 3, 1961, Inclusive* (United States Printing Office, Washington, D. C., 1961), pp. 996-997 (hereinafter cited as *Biographical Dictionary of the American Congress, 1774-1961*); Annie Doom Pickrell, *Pioneer Women of Texas* (The E. L. Steck Company, Austin *circa* 1929), pp. 375-380.
2. A. W. Terrell, Autobiography, MS., Archives, University of Texas Library.

much influence over his fellows. There can be no doubt that Hamilton's rapid rise to power and the dominant role that he played, especially during the critical Reconstruction Period, were due primarily to his prowess as an orator.

Hamilton's mastery of the art of rhetoric began during his boyhood in Alabama. Even though his educational opportunities were limited, the youth made the most of those that were available. He attended the public schools of Madison County and spent much time in the local libraries. He read widely and acquired a remarkable command of words. This asset became of major importance to him in his chosen field of the law and in politics.[3]

Hamilton's legal training began while he was serving as a clerk in the office of Hugh Ulotson, Master in Chancery in the Creek country of Alabama. Here the young apprentice had an opportunity to acquire an understanding of the fundamentals of the Common Law, as well as of the essential legal forms and documents used in the practice of law. Later he read law under the guidance of Judge David Bowen of Weldona, Alabama, near the town of Talladega. While here in 1841, Hamilton received a license to practice as a lawyer. According to a later account by his daughter Betty, her father read law under Judge Bowen, courted the Judge's daughter, became his son-in-law, and, after being admitted to the bar, his law partner.[4] That Hamilton was competent in his profession when he arrived in Texas is indicated by the recognition he quickly won among most lawyers and leading citizens of Fayette County and environs. During the brief period he practiced law in La Grange, his services must have been regarded as first-rate, for he occasionally accepted valuable slaves in payment of his fees, or as security for payment.[5]

3. Resolutions of the Travis County Bar, in Austin *Evening News,* June 8, 1875; Terrell's Autobiography.

4. Resolutions of the Travis County Bar; Pickrell, *Pioneer Women of Texas,* pp. 375-380.

5. Deed Records (Fayette County, Texas), Book D, pp. 482, 557; Book E, pp. 2, 9, 384. District Court Records (Fayette County, Texas), File No. 361 (same as Case Number); File Box Nos. 220-295, Case No. 360.

A number of factors had influenced Hamilton in his decision to move to La Grange. First, it was certainly clear to him that Texas was a new and growing State, and that it offered excellent opportunities for advancement in the legal profession. Next, an older brother, Morgan C. Hamilton, undoubtedly encouraged the younger man to join him in Texas. Morgan had prospered during the nine years he had been in Texas; among his properties was a farm near La Grange which he offered his younger brother as a home. This inducement must have been the deciding reason for A. J. Hamilton's settling there.

After living less than three years in La Grange, Hamilton made another move, one of great significance for his future— to Austin, the State Capital. Again, his brother Morgan, who had moved to Austin some time earlier and had become quite well-to-do in the community, influenced A. J.'s decision.[6] With such a dependable family connection, the younger brother was no doubt confident that he could survive, even advance, in this center of political activity and power. With the aid of his older brother, Hamilton bought the James E. Webb home and farm as a permanent dwelling place. This property was located about one and a half miles southeast of the Old Capitol,[7] a building later destroyed by fire and replaced by the present imposing structure. The State Cemetery now occupies a part of the farm.[8]

The Hamilton family at this time consisted of the father and mother and four children—Mary and Frank, born in Alabama; John, born in Fayette County; and Betty, born in a temporary home in Austin. Two additional children—Lillie

6. Pearl Cashell Jackson, *Governors' Wives* (E. L. Steck, Austin, *circa* 1915), pp. 54-63.

7. *Ibid.* Note for $1,000 dated December 18, 1850, in favor of James Webb, and signed by M. C. and A. J. Hamilton, in A. J. Hamilton papers, Archives, University of Texas Library, Austin.

8. Walter Prescott Webb and H. Bailey Carroll (eds.), *The Handbook of Texas* (2 vols., Texas State Historical Association, Austin, 1952), II, p. 661 (hereinafter cited as *Texas Handbook*); Mary Katherine Decherd, The State Cemetery, MS., Archives Division, Texas State Library, Austin.

and Katie—were to be born on the farm near the Capitol.[9] Still later—during their stay in New Orleans after the Civil War— the Hamiltons would adopt Emile, a French boy, and bring him to live with them in Austin when they returned.[10] This was a close-knit, warmly affectionate family. Hamilton delighted in joining the children in games such as charades, in dancing reels, and in group singing.

Mrs. Hamilton was tall and impressive in appearance, with sparkling eyes and a wealth of dark hair. She was said to be a woman "who dresses well, preferring fine material to showy display." Moreover, she possessed courage and managerial ability. She managed the farm to a large extent when Hamilton was at home, and altogether when he was in Congress and away during the Civil War. In spite of her husband's somewhat irregular life, she and the children regarded him with deep affection; in fact, they almost idolized him for his agreeable qualities.[11]

As already implied, the brother, Morgan Hamilton, was closely tied to the family. He was born on February 25, 1809, near Huntsville, Madison County, Alabama, where as a boy he attended the local public schools. He then engaged in the mercantile business in Alabama until he moved to Texas in 1837. In Texas, he served as a clerk in the Department of War and Marine for more than seven years. During the last three months of his employment, he was Acting Head of the Department. As a result of this service to the Republic of Texas, Morgan received liberal grants of land. To these he subsequently added thousands of acres through the purchase of land certificates and scrip.

Morgan prospered in the mercantile business in Austin for a number of years, but in 1852 he retired to devote himself

9. The A. J. Hamilton Bible, in possession of John H. Chiles, Jr., great-grandson of Hamilton, 2304 Woodlawn, Austin, Texas.

10. Interview with Frank and Bessie Woodburn, grandson and granddaughter of A. J. Hamilton, April 29, 1962.

11. Jackson, *Governors' Wives*, pp. 54-63; Mrs. E. M. Pease to Juliet Niles, April 18, 1875, in R. Niles Graham-Elisha Marshall Pease Collection, Archives, Public Library, Austin.

increasingly to public affairs.[12] His activities in this connection will be noted as the career of his brother is described in the pages that follow. Morgan, a bachelor, maintained his own apartment in Austin, but he was a frequent and welcome visitor in his brother's home. His interest in and influence on the family were important and they lasted to the time of his death.

It is possible that even before A. J. Hamilton joined his older brother in Austin, he was known in the State Capital as a competent lawyer and public speaker. At any rate, his abilities were recognized soon after he arrived, since in January, 1850, Governor P. H. Bell appointed him Acting Attorney General.[13] As it turned out, his duties were limited and of little importance; during approximately one year in office, he handled only routine matters before the State Supreme Court. Since his work was light and his salary small, he appeared on several occasions, with the aid of associate lawyers, as counsel in his own cases before the Court. Hamilton hoped to continue in office—as Attorney General—and ran for the position in the next election, held in August, 1850. But strong opposition developed from a number of prominent lawyers who lived in the eastern, more populous counties, and he was defeated.[14] Even so, he was on his way politically.

In 1851, apparently without opposition, Hamilton was elected a member of the Fourth Legislature from Travis County, in which Austin is situated. He soon became a strong and influential member of the lower house.[15] The all-important topics before the Legislature at this time were, first, the payment

12. *Biographical Dictionary of the American Congress, 1774-1961*, p. 1053; *Texas Handbook*, I, p. 760; *Abstract of Land Titles of Texas Comprising the Titles of Patented and Located Lands in the State* (Shaw & Blaylock, Galveston, 1878), I-II, *passim*.

13. Governor P. H. Bell to A. J. Hamilton, January 15, 1850, in A. J. Hamilton Papers, Archives, University of Texas Library.

14. *Reports of Cases Argued and Decided in the Supreme Court of the State of Texas* (court reporters and publishers vary). IV-V, *passim*, Archives Division, Texas State Library; State Election Returns, August 16, 1850, Archives Division, Texas State Library.

15. *Texas State Gazette* (Austin), May 3, August 9, September 13, 1851.

of the debt of the Republic of Texas and, second, internal improvements, especially railroad construction. The debt problem
engaged the attention of the legislators for many hours. A so-
called scaling plan, whereby each creditor was to receive
approximately what he had paid into the State Treasury, was
finally adopted.[16] Hamilton opposed the idea of scaling the
debt, and (somewhat like Alexander Hamilton, Secretary of
the Treasury under Washington) he fought for paying the
face value of every bond or certificate of indebtedness. He
firmly believed that the State, in order to establish its credit
in the bond markets, must pay every cent of every obligation,
including interest. In an effort to block action in favor of
scaling, or to override it, Hamilton published "An Address
to the People of Texas." which called for the State to cede to
the United States Government the north half of the Pan-
handle, approximately 15,000,000 acres, as a means of raising
the funds necessary to discharge current liabilities. He felt that
the Congress of the United States would be generous in paying for the area to be transferred. At 50 cents an acre—mentioned frequently as a reasonable price—the amount received
would have totaled $7,500,000.[17]

This approach, as Hamilton viewed it, would be attractive
both to the creditors and to the taxpayers of the State. The
money received from the cession of lands would be used to
make up the losses of the creditors of the Republic, with the
understanding that they would permit the State to use fifty
per cent of their payments to buy stock in a railroad to be
built from Central Texas to the Gulf of Mexico. Hamilton
was eloquent in his appeal to the people by asking them
if they would not be willing to "exchange a distant and cheer-
less region" in order to pay "every farthing of the revolutionary debt," thus avoiding the "stain of repudiation." In
addition, the new legislator from Travis County insisted, the
proceeds from the cession might well insure the building of

16. *Ibid.*, February 14, July 24, 1852; H. P. N. Gammel (compiler), *Laws of
Texas* (10 vols., Austin, 1898), III, p. 208.
17. *Texas State Gazette*, February 21, 1852.

a greatly needed railroad from Central Texas to the Gulf of Mexico.[18] While his proposal caused some favorable reaction in Washington, in Texas it failed to win the response Hamilton had hoped for. Perhaps the creditors of the government of Texas were reasonably content with the scaling settlement; perhaps also the railroad promoters had found what they hoped would be a satisfactory source of funds for their enterprise.[19]

As for the construction of railroads, it was clear that not enough private capital could be raised in Texas or elsewhere to underwrite such projects. Yet from the standpoint of the railroad builders, the situation was not entirely hopeless. The State Common School Fund had recently been enriched by 2,000 United States indemnity bonds, valued at $2,000,000, a sum received in payment for land along the boundary of Texas and New Mexico.[20] Why not use part of this fund as a subsidy by granting loans from it to railroad construction companies? Such a proposal was forthwith incorporated into a bill for enactment into law by the Legislature.

The advocates of the measure were so enthusiastic in their support that they overlooked the constitutional questions involved. A. J. Hamilton, on the other hand, after careful study of the bill designed to authorize loans from the Common School Fund, became convinced that the scheme was both unconstitutional and fraudulent. He concluded that the supporters of the bill sought cleverly to join education and internal improvements in the same measure—a move that violated the provision of the State Constitution requiring that a bill should contain only one subject. As those who promoted the bill well knew, a simple majority would have been sufficient to pass it as an appropriation for education. Hamilton vigorously condemned this tactic. In the course of his remarks in opposition, he declared: "Error cannot be sustained by truth,

18. *Ibid.,* February 14, 1852; January 8, 1853.

19. *Ibid.,* July 24, 1852.

20. *United States Statutes at Large* (United States Printing Office, Washington, D. C.), IX, pp. 446-447; Gammel, *Laws of Texas,* III, p. 1461.

but must look to means and arguments of a kindred nature: artfulness, duplicity, and sophistry."[21]

Hamilton's arguments must have convinced a sufficient number of members that the bill as framed was unconstitutional, for action was delayed indefinitely. This delay meant, in effect, defeat for the measure. Yet, while Hamilton won his point, he lost influential political support. Largely as a result of his opposition to the railroad-education bill, he was defeated in 1853 for reelection to the Legislature.[22] This setback, however, was not serious. On the contrary, Hamilton's reputation seems to have benefited from his forthright stand for political integrity. He was soon chosen as special counsel for the State in the important case of *Texas v. Delesdenier* (7 Tex. 76).

The action of one Delesdenier gave rise to this litigation. In 1846, he had taken by force of arms possession of land on Galveston Island that was reserved to the State. In the district court an attempt of the Attorney General to recover the land had been denied, and an appeal to the State Supreme Court followed. This case was an important one, for it concerned the power of Texas to reserve and control all islands that it claimed. The State employed Hamilton as special counsel. He prepared his brief with great care, with the result that the opinion of the Supreme Court in favor of the State was based largely on his reasoning. In payment of the notable service he had rendered, he subsequently received from the Legislature a substantial fee, $1,500.[23]

By now, A. J. Hamilton was a marked man, chiefly because of his ability as a speaker. In those pioneer days, the public greatly esteemed an accomplished orator. Hamilton possessed in a remarkable way the qualities that swayed listeners to approve and to act.[24]

His rich, even flow of words, delivered in resonant tones,

21. *Texas State Gazette,* March 22 and September 6, 1851; March 12, 1853.
22. *Ibid.,* March 12, 19, June 11, 1853.
23. Gammel, *Laws of Texas,* II, p. 53.
24. B. E. Tarver to A. J. Hamilton, July 10, 1855; J. L. Gay to A. J. Hamilton, November 1, 1856—both in A. J. Hamilton Papers, University of Texas Library.

led those who had heard Henry Clay, whose voice was "rich, musical, and captivating," to compare the Texas orator to him.[25] Hamilton's speeches in 1855 and 1857 delivered respectively in defense of W. W. Montgomery and in behalf of a Negro slave named Cuff won a place for him in the front rank of Texas criminal lawyers. An observer at the trial of Montgomery said that Hamilton "spoke with such fire, directness, and force that the jury was completely overcome," and that all who heard the speech were convinced that Hamilton was " a man of transcendent forensic genius." After attending the second trial of the slave, the same observer declared that the speech of Hamilton, "in pathos and grandeur, has been rarely equaled, and never surpassed."[26]

Hamilton was much in demand as a speaker outside the courtroom and was frequently heard on occasions such as celebrations of Washington's Birthday or Stephen F. Austin's, the arrival of the first steamboat in Austin, and open meetings of the State Supreme Court. His reputation spread; he was invited, at different times, to speak in Galveston and various other places.[27]

Hamilton was by nature convivial, and he especially enjoyed a merry feast with his family and his friends. Austin lawyers, quite often in a group on horseback, traveled the district-court circuit. Hamilton, riding a fine horse, occasionally led the way. On some such excursions, the Austin lawyers carried lunches with them, and at attractive spots along the way stopped to rest their horses, and lunched together. During these hours of relaxation Hamilton led in singing the hymns and songs popular in those days.[28]

25. Calvin Colton, *The Life and Times of Henry Clay* (2 vols., A. S. Barnes & Co., New York, 1846), I, pp. 63-64.

26. Frank Brown, Annals of Travis County and the City of Austin from the Earliest Times to the Close of 1875, Ch. 18, p. 14, MS., typescript copy, n. p., nd., Archives, University of Texas Library—hereinafter cited as Annals of Travis County).

27. *Ibid.*, Ch. 17, p. 41; William Pitt Ballinger, Diary, typescript copy, entries for June 6, 1857; November 28, 1860, Archives, University of Texas Library, Austin. *Texas State Gazette*, March 8, 1851.

28. A. W. Terrell, Autobiography, MS., Archives, University of Texas Library.

In celebration of a victory in court or in a political contest Hamilton enjoyed sipping a glass of beer with colleagues and friends. Unfortunately this predilection gradually became more than an occasional indulgence. An unfriendly editor remarked that Hamilton, "if sober," might do this, or that. The words indicated that the lawyer's taste for liquor had grown, and that it was becoming well-known.[29]

Nevertheless, Hamilton's popularity with his fellow lawyers was solidly based. They not only liked him; they also respected him. Following the death on December 8, 1856, of Abner S. Lipscomb, Associate Justice of the State Supreme Court, a large group of them appealed to Hamilton to seek the office left vacant by the death of Mr. Lipscomb. Hamilton's reaction was to start a petition addressed to O. M. Roberts—signing it first—requesting him to seek the position. Roberts complied and was duly elected.[30]

During these earlier days of his career in Austin, whether Hamilton ran for office or not, he took an active part in every campaign. The Know Nothing Party, parading in Texas as both a nationalist and a pro-slavery party, attracted the approval of many of the prominent leaders of the State, including such stalwarts as Sam Houston. Hamilton, in what seems to have been a moment of aberration, was also beguiled into a temporary association with this party. Yet, as soon as he realized what the Know Nothings really stood for, he repented this action, for their narrow nativism and intolerant religious bigotry revolted him. He not only withdrew from the party, but also openly attacked it. As a result of his opposition to the Know Nothings, he was given much credit for their defeat in Texas in 1855.[31]

29. W. P. Ballinger, Diary, entry of June 3, 1857; *State Gazette,* June 4, 1859 (clipping from Houston *Telegraph*).

30. H. W. Sublett to O. M. Roberts, December 13, 1856, January 20, 1857; A. P. Wiley to O. M. Roberts, January 8, 1857; John H. Reagan to O. M. Roberts, January 12, 1857—all in O. M. Roberts' Letters, MS., Archives, University of Texas Library; O. M. Roberts to A. J. Hamilton, December 20, 1856, in A. J. Hamilton Papers, Archives, University of Texas Library.

31. Dudley G. Wooten (ed.), *A Comprehensive History of Texas, 1685-1897* (2 vols., W. G. Scarff, Dallas, 1898), II, Part III (written by O. M. Roberts),

Hamilton's brief association with the Know Nothings was not a break with, or abandonment of, the Democratic Party, a fact that was recognized by its leaders. In a subsequent Democratic convention, held in 1858, Hamilton and several other backsliders were restored to good fellowship in the ranks during somewhat hilarious proceedings. Each offender, escorted by a Democratic sponsor, was led into the convention hall and down to the stage, where he was presented as a redeemed sinner to the amused faithful. This action was patterned on that of the Methodist Church during this period. If a member fell from grace, he was escorted to the "Mourners' Bench" where, after confession of error, he was restored to good standing.[32]

As a Democrat, Hamilton was individualistic in personality and independent in thinking; consequently, he was never an enthusiastic organization man. Even though the party named him a presidential elector in 1856, he was never committed to partisan objectives beyond his personal conscience and judgment.[33] It is true that Hamilton became a devoted Texan, but it is also true that he was never a sectionalist. When he referred to the constitution, unless he specifically indicated otherwise, he spoke of the Constitution of the United States; with him, the flag was always the Star-Spangled Banner.

It is evident that Hamilton absorbed this spirit of nationalism from his father, James Hamilton, who had served as a captain of frontier militia under Andrew Jackson during the Creek Indian Wars. Jackson's victories with his militiamen contributed greatly to the rising spirit of nationalism that characterized the period immediately following the War of 1812. It is well to note that James Hamilton named his son "Andrew Jackson" for the famous Tennessean, and that the

pp. 32, 53-54; *Southern Intelligencer* (Austin), May 25, 1859 (clipping from San Antonio *Zeitung*).

32. Frank Brown, Annals of Travis County, Ch. 17, p. 48; *State Gazette,* July 18, 1855.

33. *Ibid.,* May 3, 1856; *Dallas Herald,* June 7, 1856 (clipping from *Waco Statesman*); Ernest William Winkler (ed.), *Platforms of Political Parties in Texas* (Bulletin of the University of Texas, 1916, No. 53), pp. 64-65.

son in time demonstrated many of the characteristics of the man whose name he bore.

As he matured, A. J. Hamilton developed through association with his father, an independent farmer, a sense of appreciation and respect for farmers and working people as a class. The elder Hamilton and his wife, Jane Bayless Hamilton, were rugged pioneers who settled on Indian lands in Madison County, Mississippi Territory, before they were ceded to the United States. During the first public sale, after these lands had been acquired by treaty, James Hamilton bought 160 acres (SE ¼, Sec. 6, Township 3 South, Range 2 East, Huntsville Meridian). Though never a member of the slave-owning planter class, he obtained in excess of nine hundred acres of farmland, and became a successful farmer. Apparently, he and his own children provided the labor on the farm. A. J. Hamilton, like his father, took pride in the ownership of land and in its productivity.[34]

Such a sincere nationalist as A. J. Hamilton could not avoid the political tensions that prevailed in Texas during the 1850's. As these tensions mounted over the issue of slavery, a movement was begun in the Democratic Party to achieve greater discipline among its members in support of slavery and Southern rights. The leader of this movement was John Marshall, militant editor of the *State Gazette,* published in Austin. In the State Democratic Convention of 1857, Marshall and his supporters secured the adoption of a platform strongly pro-slavery in its emphasis. They were able also to bring

34. Dunbar Rowland, "Mississippi Territory in the War of 1812," *Publications of the Mississippi Historical Society,* IV, pp. 189-193; Thomas Jones Taylor, "Early History of Madison County and Incidentals of North Alabama," *Alabama Historical Quarterly,* Vol. I, pp. 71, 161, 313 (courtesy of Peter A. Brannon, Director Department of Archives and History, Capitol Building, Montgomery, to J. L. Waller, December 17, 1962); Clarence Edwin Carter (ed.), *United States Department of State: Territorial Papers of the United States: Alabama and Mississippi, 1796-1817* (United States Printing Office, Washington, D.C., 1934-_____), V, pp. 685, 720, 725; *ibid.,* VI, pp. 227, 613, Alabama State Land Tract Book, p. 212, Office of the Secretary of State, Capitol Building, Montgomery; Madison County Estates Records (typescript copy in Alabama State Archives, Montgomery), Vol. 113, p. 72; Vol. 115, p. 72; Vol. 137, p. 28; Vol. 73, p. 94.

about the nomination of Hardin R. Runnels for Governor and Francis R. Lubbock for Lieutenant Governor, both fully committed to a policy of extremism regarding Southern rights. In the election that followed, Runnels, though opposed by prestigious Sam Houston, won decisively—by a vote of 32,552 to 23,628. Editor Marshall, in effect, shouted the results of the election from the housetops and was awarded a contract for all the State printing for his efforts. Now Chairman of the Democratic State Committee, he urged that all candidates for State office be nominated by conventions, and the committee supported the plan.[35]

As a result of this change of procedure, a Democratic political convention in the spring of 1858 nominated District Judge C. W. Buckley for Associate Justice of the Texas State Supreme Court. But to counter the powerful and influential *State Gazette,* a new publication, the *Southern Intelligencer,* which had been established in 1856 and was being published in Austin, came out in opposition. The editor, George W. Paschal, believed that judges should be free from political influence; he therefore persuaded Judge James H. Bell of the First Judicial District to run against Buckley.[36]

The contest between Bell and Buckley confronted Hamilton with a fateful decision. Though a year earlier (in 1857) he had favored the nomination of another candidate for Governor, Hamilton had voted for Runnels. Soon, however, he became alarmed by the extreme demands of Governor Runnels for congressional safeguards for Southern rights, with implications of secession unless they were established. Hamilton was now obliged to decide whether an associate justice should be chosen on the basis of a political nomination. Like Editor Paschal, Hamilton was convinced that Supreme Court justices

35. *State Gazette,* August 25, October 13, 1855; November 12, 1856; February 4, September 30, November 25, December 2 and 26, 1857; August 4, 1858; Winkler, *Platforms of Political Parties in Texas,* p. 72.

36. *State Gazette,* May 16, 1857; January 23, March 6, August 21, 1858; *Southern Intelligencer,* February 21, November 25, December 23, 1857; August 4 and 25, 1858.

should be free from partisan influence.[37] How could he maintain his self-respect if he acceded to this questionable political act? By the summer of 1858, he had become restive to the point of rebellion.

On July 31 in Austin, before an overflowing, wildly enthusiastic crowd in one of the most colorful speeches of his life—the dramatic "chinkapin, popcorn, goober pea" speech—Hamilton broke with the State Democratic organization, and came out in support of James H. Bell for Associate Justice of the Supreme Court, in opposition to Judge C. W. Buckley, the convention nominee.[38] The occasion was marked by unusual anticipation and excitement, for rumors had spread that Hamilton would openly attack the State Democratic organization. This he did without mincing words. He directed his immediate remarks against the so-called "Austin Clique," composed of Editor John Marshall, the top administrative officers of the State, the Democratic State Committee, and others. He bitterly denounced these leaders, who, he felt, expected to get their rewards from the State Treasury. In the course of his invective, Hamilton shouted: "Let's organize! Here's the public treasury for the organs, organizers, organ grinders."[39] The *Southern Intelligencer,* probably Editor George W. Paschal, wrote a vivid description of Hamilton in action and a comprehensive digest of his speech. After commenting on Hamilton's good health and happy mood, the newspaper observed: "His stalwart figure and his Jupiter voice mark him as a democrat, stamped with the proud man's patent. His strength and frame were gained" by honest work on his father's farm, "which the silk-stocking gentry think degrading to all but the Negro." The account went on to describe the speech as the "effort of Hamilton's life . . . the soaring of the proud eagle which feels its independence," marked by the

37. *Ibid.,* November 25 and December 23, 1857; January 6, July 28, August 4 and 25, 1858; *State Gazette,* December 25, 1857; January 23, March 6, August 21, 1858; Winkler, *Platforms of Political Parties in Texas,* p. 75.
38. *Southern Intelligencer,* August 4, 1858; *State Gazette,* August 21, 1858.
39. *Ibid.,* August 14, 1858; *Southern Intelligencer,* August 4, 1858.

dedication of one who had chosen the "thorny path of duty."[40]

Following Hamilton's address, the leaders of the Democratic organization charged him with base ingratitude to the party that had honored him. They called him a "political eel," that is, a slippery politician without principles. Yet Hamilton and his friends insisted that he was a firm believer in true Democratic principles—the Jeffersonian principles of freedom of speech and of the press, of personal liberty, and of the right of voters freely to choose their officials.[41]

During 1858 and 1859 the slavery issue became more and more disturbing. Editor Marshall of the *State Gazette,* as well as other militant editors in Texas, assumed an increasingly aggressive position on slavery. Marshall asserted that slavery was not only recognized in the Constitution of the United States but it was also sanctioned by the Bible and was blessed of God. Sure of his position, he began to advocate the reopening of the African slave trade—a trade that had been outlawed by the entire Western world, including the United States.[42] At this time, Hamilton did not oppose the institution of slavery as such, as shown by his ownership of two or three slaves in the 1850's, but he did oppose reopening the African slave trade.[43]

The influence of these extreme Southerners in Texas was so strong that the pro-slavery Runnels was renominated by the Democrats—and this in spite of considerable criticism of his neglect of frontier defense and his excessive absence from office. The *Southern Intelligencer* called upon Sam Houston to oppose the reelection of Runnels. Houston responded readily and ran on a platform of maintaining the Constitution of the United States and preserving the Union. In a bitter campaign, he declared that Runnels possessed all the qualities of a dog, except fidelity. Houston had consistent-

40. Same sources as in reference 39 above.
41. *State Gazette,* August 14 and 21, 1858; June 4, 1859; *Southern Intelligencer,* June 11, 1859.
42. *State Gazette,* February 12 and 16, 1859.
43. Tax Rolls, Travis County, Texas, 1851, 1852, 1854.

ly condemned the African slave trade; he now insisted that it was the central issue of the election.[44]

Meanwhile, A. J. Hamilton was neither inactive nor forgotten. In the spring of 1859, a San Antonio leader, John A. Wilcox, had endorsed Hamilton—"Colossal Hamilton," he called the big Texan—as a suitable candidate for Congress.[45] Shortly thereafter, on May 21, 1859, before an enthusiastic audience in Austin, Hamilton announced his candidacy for Congress from the Western District of Texas. He indicated that he would run as an Independent Democrat and would support the Cincinnati Platform of 1856, upon which Buchanan had been elected President of the United States. In the course of his remarks, Hamilton charged that the Democratic convention that had renominated Runnels and Lubbock had violated the pledge not to renew agitation. He also insisted that the pro-Southern leaders of the party were attempting to reopen the African slave trade. He denounced this objective and other extreme demands as a screen for secession and disunion. He went on to say that, contrary to the views of some, it was not degrading for whites to work in the fields. In an eloquent passage that won loud applause, he recounted the life of his family as farm workers in Alabama. Then, in conclusion, he appealed strongly for the election of Sam Houston as Governor.[46]

The *Southern Intelligencer* praised the speech, saying that it could have been delivered only by Hamilton, and by him only when supporting the great cause of free speech and the right of free men to choose without restriction their officials at the polls. Yet, not all editors agreed with the newspaper. Editor Lypssey of the *Matagorda Gazette*, commenting on Hamilton's farm work, referred to him as "a dirty-faced,

44. *Southern Intelligencer*, issues of March and April, 1859; May 25 and June 8, 1859; *State Gazette*, February 12, 19, 26, 1859; *Texas Republican* (Marshall, Texas), December 1, 1860; *Quarterly of the Texas State Historical Association*, VI, p. 155; Edward P. Maher, "Sam Houston and Secession," *Southwestern Historical Quarterly*, LV, p. 450.
45. *Southern Intelligencer*, March 9, May 25, 1859; Winkler, *Platforms of Political Parties in Texas*, pp. 77-78.
46. *Southern Intelligencer*, May 11, 25, 1859.

gnat-bitten boy, hoeing a row of potatoes side by side with his venerable sire," and asserted that his "corn-field boasting," though possibly appealing to the ignorant tenants in Alabama, would never win support among the intelligent people of Texas.[47]

The Democratic convention had nominated Thomas N. Waul as Hamilton's opponent for the seat in Congress. As the election neared, the two candidates agreed to appear in a series of joint debates, adopting the plan used in the famous debates between Abraham Lincoln and Stephen A. Douglas in 1858. Surprisingly, Waul proved to be an exceptionally strong opponent for "Colossal Jack," as Hamilton was now called. Waul contended that Hamilton was basically inconsistent and weak; that he was chronically prone to meanderings and shiftings in his politics. As a case in point, Waul repeatedly referred to Hamilton's membership in the Know Nothing Party, to which Waul had never belonged. This accusation was intended to weaken Hamilton's appeal to the influential German vote in the congressional district. In reply, Hamilton freely admitted his temporary association with the Know Nothings, but insisted that he had left them promptly on learning of their nativism and religious bigotry.

As for his opponent, Hamilton charged that Waul was committed by the platform of the State Democratic Convention, and by the extreme element of the party, to demand recklessly the reopening of the African slave trade—committed in fact, to objectives that would lead to secession and the disruption of the greatest nation on earth. Waul denied that he was pledged to a policy of extremism, but he did say that if elected he would work for the enactment of effective legislation to protect Southern rights.

Hamilton had become convinced that all forms of extremism were dangerous. Believing that a majority of the people in the congressional district agreed with him, he belabored Waul as an extremist, and kept this characterization of his opponent constantly before the voters. In evaluat-

47. *Matagorda Gazette* (Corpus Christi, Texas), June 15, 1859.

ing these exchanges, one commentator declared rather truth-
fully that as a campaigner Hamilton never gave an opponent
an advantage—and once having gained one himself, he never
gave it up.[48]

The series of debates ended in Austin, July 23, 1859, before
a large and lively audience in which there were many women.
Waul delivered the opening speech. Hamilton replied with his
usual oratorical power, concluding with a rousing appeal in
behalf of Sam Houston. The election resulted in victory for
both Houston and Hamilton. Houston won over Runnels by
a vote of 36,257 to 27,500. Hamilton's victory was closer but
safe enough: he received 16,840 votes to Waul's 15,583.[49]
Supporters of the Congressman-elect were greatly pleased
with the outcome. They praised Hamilton as a statesman of
whom great things were expected. In the words of the *Southern Intelligencer*: "Hamilton is able to stand among the tal-
lest in the nation, as an orator and man of genius . . . He is
self-made, independent and self-reliant . . . He will be
no dummy in Congress—no carpet knight, but soldier and
orator."[50]

48. *State Gazette,* June 4, 18, 1859; *Southern Intelligencer,* May 25, June 11
and 18, 1859.
49. *Ibid.,* May 25 and July 27, 1859; *Texas Almanac,* 1960, p. 215.
50. *Southern Intelligencer,* May 25, 1859.

CHAPTER II

Texas Unionist in Congress

THE THIRTY-SIXTH CONGRESS assembled on December 5, 1859, in Washington, D.C., at a time of confusion and stress throughout the nation. A. J. Hamilton did not answer the first roll call but did take his seat the next day.[1] He and other members of the Congress were much concerned with the tensions that prevailed. On December 2, three days before the Congress convened, John Brown had been hanged for "murder, criminal conspiracy, and treason against the Commonwealth of Virginia" as a result of his reckless raid the preceding October 16.[2]

The Republican Party in Congress was united and confident. Since its organization in 1854, it had made rapid gains. With support of the Free-Soil Democrats, the Republican Congressmen were in a position to elect the Speaker and control the activities of the current session. The South as a whole was alarmed at the possibility that a "Black Republican" Speaker would be chosen, and many congressmen from different parts of the country opposed the idea.[3] Southern congressmen were inclined to regard with distrust many of their Democratic colleagues from the North, especially those who had opposed the admission of Kansas under the Lecompton Constitution, which was pro-slavery.

On the first eleven ballots cast in electing the Speaker, A. J. Hamilton voted for Thomas S. Bocock of Virginia. In the

1. *The Congressional Globe: The Debates and Proceedings* (The Congressional Globe Office, Washington, D.C., 46 vols. in 109, from December 2, 1834 to March 3, 1873), 1861, 36th Cong., 1st Sess., Pt. I, p. 40.
2. Samuel Eliot Morison and Henry Steele Commager, *The Growth of the American Republic* (2 vols., Oxford Press, New York, 1950), I, p. 633.
3. Roy F. Nichols, *The Disruption of American Democracy* (Macmillan, New York, 1948), pp. 10, 18, 48, 100, 171-174, 202, 272; Allan Nevins, *The Emergence of Lincoln* (2 vols., Charles Scribner's Sons, New York, 1950), I, pp. 234-235.

interest of harmony within the Democratic Party and with the objective of maintaining the Union, he joined his congressional colleague from Texas, John H. Reagan, on the next few ballots; they voted several times for John A. McClernand of Illinois, an anti-Lecompton Democrat.[4] On other ballots, the two Texans voted for Alexander R. Boteler of Virginia, Horace Maynard of Tennessee, Charles L. Scot of California, and McClernand, respectively.[5]

The twenty-ninth ballot for Speaker produced an astonishing result: Hamilton himself received 89 votes, to 103 for John Sherman of Ohio. Also on this ballot there was a courtesy vote of fourteen for John A. Gilmer of North Carolina, with a scattering of five other votes. A shift of these nineteen votes to Hamilton would have made him Speaker; in view of the feelings of the Southern members who feared that Sherman would be elected, it is puzzling that the shift was not made. James L. Pugh of Alabama and James M. Leach of North Carolina, both members of the American Party, voted for Hamilton and appealed to all except Republicans to unite in supporting him for Speaker.[6]

The appeal by Pugh and Leach, however, failed, and the 89 votes cast for Hamilton on the twenty-ninth ballot were the largest number that he received at any time. Even so, for the next four ballots, after which Hamilton withdrew his name, he continued to receive strong support.[7]

What is the explanation of this remarkable vote accorded a freshman congressman from faraway Texas? Perhaps Hamilton's reputation as an orator was known to many of his congressional colleagues. Perhaps, also, he had already met and favorably impressed a number of his colleagues, since he possessed the appearance and personality with which great statesmen of that era were supposed to be endowed.

4. *Ibid.,* I, pp. 251, 274, 357-359, 401; II, pp. 52, 63-65, 116-119; *Congressional Globe,* 36th Cong., 1st Sess., Pt. I, pp. 197, 360.
5. *Ibid.,* 1st Sess., Pt. I, pp. 52, 87, 158, 165, 170, 175, 188, 197, 235, 274, 338, 360.
6. *Ibid.,* p. 373.
7. *Ibid.,* pp. 408-409.

Some supporters may have been influenced by more practical considerations: the fact that Hamilton had broken with the Texas State Democratic organization and had been elected as an Independent Unionist; and the fact that he defended the Union and insisted that Texas must remain a part of it. Such considerations, however, proved ineffective. On the forty-third ballot William Pennington of New Jersey was elected Speaker; and the House of the Thirty-sixth Congress was finally organized.[8]

Hamilton withdrew his name as a candidate for the Speakership in an address which he delivered, January 26, 1860. While expressing his appreciation for the remarkable vote that his colleagues had accorded him, he explained his position regarding the Union:

Much has been said of the Union and love of the Union on the one hand and dissolution of the Union on the other . . . The Union, sir, is being dissolved now. It may be in the power of the conservative elements of this House to arrest it; but that cannot be done by the election of a Black Republican Speaker. I believe that I represent as conservative a constituency as any gentleman upon this floor; a people who are devoted to the Union; a people, sir, who have, I think, manifested that devotion by as much liberality and unselfishness, by yielding up what no other State in the Union has yielded, a separate nationality, in order to participate in the Confederacy which we all profess so much to love; and yet that same State, that same people are now solemnly resolving that it is better that the wheels of Government should be arrested where they are today, and no organization ever effected, than that the candidate of the Republican Party shall be elected and placed in the Speaker's chair.[9]

After learning of this speech, Editor Marshall of the *State Gazette* (Texas) found nothing to praise in Hamilton's plea for the preservation of the Union. Instead, he declared that Hamilton's life was a "record of weaknesses and inconsistencies," and that his greatest ambition was to "establish his capacity to make a good speech upon every side of every subject."[10] This vituperation showed clearly that Marshall re-

8. *Ibid.,* p. 650.
9. *Ibid.,* pp. 603-604.
10. *State Gazettte,* September 22, 1860.

mained bitter and unforgiving because of Hamilton's break with the State Democratic Party organization.

Hamilton was exceptionally active from the beginning of his term in the Congress. The phenomenal vote which he had received for the office of Speaker seemed to broaden his interest in national problems and increase his confidence in facing them. On February 9, 1860, he protested his assignment to the Committee on Public Lands, explaining there were no public lands of the United States in Texas.[11] On February 16, he introduced a resolution that must have appeared rather brash: it would have repealed all indirect taxes, including the tariff, in spite of the fact that the tariff had long been accepted, even by the Democratic Party, as an essential source of revenue.[12] Meanwhile, Hamilton gave due attention to the needs of his constituency in Texas: he sought appropriations for Federal courthouses in the towns of Tyler and Austin, introducing a bill for this purpose on March 7. It was read the first and the second times, and referred to the Judiciary Committee. However, the secession of Texas before the adjourment of the Thirty-sixth Congress ended the matter.[13]

While a member of Congress, Hamilton gave special consideration to problems of interest to the people of Texas. Frontier protection, especially along the Rio Grande, was the most pressing problem confronting the State in the spring of 1860. As a result of disturbances along the Border, Editor George W. Paschal of the *Southern Intelligencer* wrote Hamilton that Texas was in effect at war with Mexico.[14] The Texas-Mexican frontier was a long one, and the United States Government was charged with the duty of defending it. All during the 1850's, however, the authorities at Washington assigned only a limited number of troops to the area, and

11. *Congressional Globe,* 36th Cong., 1st Sess., Pt. I, p. 727
12. *Ibid.,* p. 813.
13. *Ibid.,* Pt. II, p. 1026; Richard B. Hubbard to Guy M. Bryan, January 19, 1858, in Guy M. Bryan Papers, Archives, University of Texas Library.
14. George W. Paschal to A. J. Hamilton, February 17, 1860, in A. J. Hamilton Papers, Archives, University of Texas Library.

Texas militiamen had to assume the major part of the responsibility. Although Hamilton attempted to induce Congress to reimburse Texas for the expenses it had incurred since February 28, 1855, in the defense of its borders, he was unable to accomplish his purpose.[15]

Governor Sam Houston, in his correspondence with Hamilton, suggested that Texas militiamen be enrolled in the United States Army, thus relieving the State of the expense of maintaining them. He also urged that the Congress make further appropriations to defray the cost of defending the frontier. Finally, Houston requested Hamilton to use his influence with the War Department in behalf of a treaty with the troublesome Indians.[16] Hamilton worked hard on these projects, but secession abruptly ended all prospects of his succeeding with them.

At the same time, Hamilton directed his attention to other projects. On May 29, 1860, he delivered an address on the Pacific Railroad Bill. In effect, Congress had already committed the nation to a subsidy for a transcontinental railroad, having appropriated money for surveys of five possible routes. If the promoters could realize their hopes, a veritable stream of commerce would flow over the Pacific Railroad. This flow of trade would materially increase the prosperity of the large cities and section nearest the eastern terminus of the transcontinental span. Jefferson Davis, under whose supervision the surveys were made, recommended following the southern route in constructing the line westward. This proposal by a Mississippian raised serious sectional issues.

A. J. Hamilton, a Texan, was in favor of a congressional subsidy for the railroad, but he did not want Texas and the

15. *U.S. Statutes at Large* (United States Printing Office, Washington, D.C.), X, pp. 617-619.

16. Governor Sam Houston to Congressman A. J. Hamilton, March 17, 1860, in Amelia E. Williams and Eugene C. Barker (eds.), *Writings of Sam Houston* (8 vols., Texas State Historical Association, Austin, 1943), VII, p. 526; A. J. Hamilton to Governor Houston, June 30, 1860, in *ibid.,* VIII, p. 22; U. S. Secretary of War John Floyd to his Second Auditor, November 15, 1860 (copy in Governors' Correspondence—Houston—Archives, Texas State Library).

South ignored in fixing either the route or the eastern terminus of the line. He therefore argued for the building of two roads— to follow the southern and northern routes, respectively. He believed that if the need for both were not immediate, it would soon develop. By anticipating this need, both the North and the South would be satisfied and benefited.

But as the discussion of these ideas proceeded, Hamilton became convinced that they were unacceptable to many of his colleagues in the House of Representatives. As a result, he became aroused and resentful. When his emotions were stirred, the Congressman from Texas was apt to use strong language and to question the sincerity of his opponents. In a bitter speech, he declared that the South had been a beggar too long. All that the South expected, he continued, was right and justice; and he rather belligerently asserted that it would be gained one way or another. Back in Texas, these intemperate remarks were not favorably received by everyone, in spite of Hamilton's intention to defend the interests of the State. Thus the *Texas Republican,* instead of bestowing praise on him, accused Hamilton of inconsistency with sentiments he had expressed earlier.[17]

As the clouds of intersectional conflict gathered in those first months of 1860, Hamilton must have viewed the portents with alarm. During April the presidential nominating convention of the Democratic Party met in Charleston, South Carolina, a hotbed of secession sentiment. The convention soon broke up over the adoption of a party platform. Stephen A. Douglas of Illinois controlled a majority of the delegates; they voted to adopt the minority report of the platform committee. This report favored Douglas' position on slavery, which would have permitted the territorial legislatures to decide the issue in their respective areas. The Southern Democrats had consistently maintained that Congress itself should protect the institution of slavery in the territories; they bolted the conven-

17. *Congressional Globe,* 36th Cong., 1st Sess., Pt. III, pp. 2445-2448; *Texas Republican* (Marshall, Texas), December 15, 1860.

tion when they realized that it would not support their position.

Since Douglas did not command the two-thirds majority necessary at that time for nomination as the presidential candidate, he and his supporters adjourned to Baltimore. There, the Northern Democrats, failing to persuade the Southern bolters to return to the convention, in short order nominated Douglas. The bolters, in their turn, meeting in Richmond, Virginia, chose John C. Breckinridge of Kentucky as their candidate. To complicate matters further, a group calling themselves the Constitutional Union Party—mostly former Whigs and Know Nothings—assembled in Baltimore and nominated John Bell of Tennessee for the presidency.

In the meantime, a confident Republican convention met in Chicago and nominated Abraham Lincoln of Illinois as the standard-bearer of the newly organized and dynamic party. Although Lincoln had become known throughout the nation because of the famous Lincoln-Douglas debates of 1858, he was wholly unacceptable to the defenders of slavery. His "House Divided" speech had alienated pro-slavery elements by predicting that the country would eventually become all slave or all free.[18]

On May 4, Hamilton wrote his wife that he was eager to return home to Texas. He had taken his three eldest children— Mary, Frank, and John—with him to Washington and placed them in school. He told his wife that he would bring "Spunky," their pet-name for Mary, with him.[19] Congress adjourned on June 18, and Hamilton probably arrived in Austin early in July.

An address that he delivered soon after his arrival was reported in the *State Gazette* of July 28. In it, he roundly critized the actions of the Democrats at Charleston, Richmond, and Baltimore. Moreover, he predicted that Lincoln would

18. Ralph Volney Harlow, *The United States: From Wilderness to World Power* (Henry Holt, New York, 1949), pp. 327-328; *State Gazette,* October 6, pp. 13, 27, 1860.

19. A. J. Hamilton to his wife, Mary, May 6, June 4, 1860, in A. J. Hamilton Papers, Archives, University of Texas Library.

be elected unless the Democrats could and would close ranks. To avoid defeat, he urged his fellow party members to unite in support of the Stephen A. Douglas - Herschel V. Johnson ticket. In this effort at unity, E. M. Pease and others joined Hamilton in an appeal to the voters of Texas, and inferentially to those of the South.[20]

Hamilton's prediction of the outcome of the presidential election proved to be correct. The movement to assemble a State convention, which was under way even before Lincoln's election, encountered a roadblock in Governor Houston. He feared that such a convention would adopt an ordinance of secession that in turn would lead to war and the defeat and humiliation of the South. Nevertheless, the convention movement was gaining momentum at the time Hamilton left Austin to attend the second session of the Thirty-sixth Congress.[21]

The leaders of the movement devised a plan that bypassed Governor Houston with the result that a State convention assembled in Austin, January 28, 1861. It promptly organized and elected O. M. Roberts as president. He proceeded at once to appoint a committee charged with drafting an Ordinance of Secession and a Declaration of Causes.[22] The latter document expressed a number of grievances, somewhat general in nature, against the leaders of the Federal government. It contained such accusations as their unfriendly attitude toward the South, their invoking a "higher law" than the Constitution, their spreading of seditious literature through the mails, and their failing to protect the frontier. The declaration, however, included no catalogue of offenses against the people; and, of more importance, in the event of the success of seces-

20. *State Gazette,* July 28, 1860; *True Issue* (LaGrange, Texas), October 4, 1860.

21. *Southern Intelligencer,* September 5, 1860; Robert P. Felgar, "Texas in the War for Southern Independence " (Ph.D. dissertation, University of Texas, 1935), pp. 24-26; John H. Reagan to O. M. Roberts, November 5, December 7, 1860; Gel McKay to O. M. Roberts, December 26, 1860—all in O. M. Roberts' Letters, Archives, University of Texas Library.

22. Ernest William Winkler (ed.), *Journal of the Secession Convention* (Austin Printing Company, 1912), pp. 15-17, 18-22, 61-64.

sion, it offered no real promise of advancement, prosperity, and happiness for them.[23] A number of delegates opposed submitting this revolutionary document to a vote of the people.[24] But Roberts, seconded by John H. Reagan, disagreed. They believed that the decision of the convention must be approved by the people or the leaders would be subject to the charge of usurping power. A majority of the delegates supported this view.[25]

The convention, after meeting only a few days, approved the Ordinance of Secession and the Declaration of Causes on February 1.[26] Because of the urgency of the crisis, a vote of the people on the ordinance was to be taken February 23; the returns were to be in Austin by March 1. Thus, less than thirty days was allowed for presenting the ordinance to the people, counting the votes, and making the returns.[27] On February 4, the convention, after choosing a Committee of Public Safety, adjourned to March 2.[28]

This committee, taking its role seriously, began to function without delay. It entered into negotiations with General David E. Twiggs for the surrender of the Federal forces in Texas, some 2,700 men stationed in San Antonio and at other points. The details of this grandiose bluff have been told many times. When Twiggs suggested waiting until after the people had voted, Ben McCulloch, Ranger captain, United States marshal, and later a Confederate officer, was ordered to collect a sort of demonstration force, consisting of some five hundred to one thousand volunteers. Apparently only half of them went to San Antonio, but Twiggs offered no resistance; he readily

23. *Ibid.*, pp. 48, 61-65; William Curry Holden, "Frontier Problems and Movements in West Texas, 1840-1900" (Ph.D. dissertation, University of Texas, 1928), pp. 73-74.

24. Winkler (ed.), *Journal of the Secession Convention*, pp. 61-67, 254.

25. John H. Reagan to O. M. Roberts, November 11, 1860. in O. M. Roberts' Letters, Archives, University of Texas Library.

26. Winkler (ed.), *Journal of the Secession Convention*, p. 408.

27. *Ibid.*, p. 38.

28. *Ibid.*, p. 85.

turned over his post and equipment to his challengers.[29] According to a contemporary rumor, Twiggs said that he would have surrendered to any old woman with a broom if she had demanded it in the name of Texas. His was a shameful act, and the fact that the Legislature later pronounced it patriotic and designated him a patriot does not change the truth.[30]

The Secession Convention reassembled on March 2 to canvass the returns of the election of February 23. Finding the Ordinance of Secession approved, by a vote of 46,129 for and 14,697 against, the convention proclaimed secession accomplished.[31] War now appeared to be inevitable.

Hamilton had meanwhile returned to Washington and resumed his duties in Congress. On January 18, 1861, he was able to win acceptance of an amendment to the army bill providing for an appropriation of $1,530,318.06 for maintaining a regiment of mounted volunteers in defense of the frontier of Texas. Congressman John Sherman of Ohio, as leader of the Republicans, gave Hamilton strong support in behalf of the appropriation.[32] In spite of Hamilton's success at this point, the secession of Texas rendered his efforts fruitless.[33]

Perhaps Hamilton's most important role in Congress was his service on the House Committee of Thirty-three, created in the hope of finding a solution to the crisis confronting the nation. The efforts of this committee to effect a compromise between North and South were the last desperate attempt of Congress to avoid secession and war. The Republican plat-

29. *Ibid.*, pp. 274-296; *War of the Rebellion, Official Records of the Union and Confederate Armies* (130 vols., Washington, D.C., 1880-1901), Ser. I, Vol. I, pp. 503-515; Jack W. Gunn, "Ben McCulloch: A Big Captain," *Southwestern Historical Quarterly*, LVIII, p. 18; for explanation of the action of the subcommittee, see Mary Owen Meredith, "The Life and Work of Thomas Jefferson Devine" (M.A. thesis, University of Texas, 1930), Appendix C.
30. J. K. P. Blackburn, *Reminiscences of Terry's Rangers* (Pamphlet in Austin, Texas, Public Library), p. 2; Gammel (comp.), *Laws of Texas* (10 vols., Austin, 1898), V, pp. 60, 396.
31. Winkler (ed.), *Journal of the Secession Convention*, pp. 87-88.
32. *Congressional Globe*, 36 Cong., 2nd Sess., Pt. I, p. 462.
33. *State Gazette*, December 1, 1860, March 2, 1861; *Southern Intelligencer*, March 20, 1861.

form on which Lincoln had been elected President opposed the further extension of slavery in the territories. The abolitionists of the North demanded the end of slavery, and the extreme defenders of slavery in the South demanded additional safeguards for it.

To resolve this conflict, Hamilton proposed to the Committee of Thirty-three that the domestic slave trade—that is, the selling of slaves across state lines in the South—be protected according to the plan of Congressman Charles Francis Adams who had urged that the Constitution be amended to require that any legislative act dealing with slavery must originate with some member of Congress from a slave State. Hamilton felt that if assurance could be given that Congress would never use its control over interstate commerce to interfere with the domestic slave trade, the excitement convulsing the South would be allayed.[34]

On February 1, 1861, Hamilton spoke in Congress relative to the Report of the Committee of Thirty-three on the State of the Nation. In the florid oratorical style of the day, he pledged unyielding loyalty to the Union. The peroration of his address deserves quotation in full, since it reveals Hamilton's stature as orator and statesman during the worst crisis in American history.

In traveling hither from my home, more than two thousand miles distant, for this capitol for the discharge of a public duty, my foot pressed no spot of foreign territory. My eye rested upon not one material object, during my journey, that was not a part and parcel of my country, as I fondly deemed it. When we assembled together, as far as I know, every state and territory was represented upon this floor. The great fabric of the Government was then complete; but now how changed! When I go hence, it will be to find my pathway intercepted by new and strange nationalities. Without ever having wandered from my native land, I must traverse foreign countries if I would return.

I might be excused for doubting my own identity. Surely I may be pardoned for having involuntarily prayed that this might prove a trou-

34. Martin B. Duberman, *Charles Francis Adams, 1807-1866* (Houghton, Mifflin Company, Boston, 1961), pp. 240-243; *Congressional Globe,* 36th Cong., 2nd Sess., Pt. I, Appendix, pp. 174-180.

bled and protracted dream. Yet it is too true—too many evidences force
conviction of the sad reality. But a few days past, Mr. Speaker, the noble
temple of American liberty stood complete in all its parts—stood in all
the majesty of its vast proportions, and in the glory of its apparent
strength and beauty of construction; not a pillar missing or joint dis-
severed. And its votaries were gathered about the altar worshipping, as
was their wont, with hopeful hearts. Forebodings were felt, and pre-
dictions made of the coming storm and destruction of the temple. And
the storm has come and still rages—the temple still stands, but shorn of
its fair proportions and marred in its beauty. Pillar after pillar has fallen
away. And while its proud dome still points to Heaven, it is reeling in
mid air like a drunken man, while its solid foundations are shaken as with
an earthquake.

Yet there are worshippers there, about the shrine, and I am among
them. I have been called by warning voices to come out and escape the
impending danger—I have been wooed by entreaties and plied by threats.
But, sir, neither entreaties nor threats, nor hope of reward or dread of
danger shall tear me away until I lay hold of the altar of my country,
and implore Heaven in its own good time to still this storm of civil
strife, and through such human agency as may be best, again uprear the
fallen pillars to their original position, that they may, through long ages,
contribute to strength and beauty of the noblest structure yet devised by
man.[35]

This speech marked an important turning point in Hamilton's career. By pledging his support of the Constitution, he
committed himself to oppose its enemies. Such hostile elements
had already assumed power in Texas and had made secession a fact.

Facing an uncertain future when the second session of the
Thirty-sixth Congress ended on March 2, 1861, Hamilton began the long trip back to Austin.[36] He arrived about the middle
of March, and soon afterwards delivered a bitter criticism of secession and the secessionists. He charged that the Texas Secession Convention had been assembled illegally, that its actions
were unconstitutional and revolutionary, and that the Secession
Ordinance was approved through the use of threats and by
means of indecent haste. Making this declaration at the very

35. *Ibid.*, conclusion of Hamilton's speech to Committee of Thirty-three.
36. *Ibid.*, 2nd Ses., Pt. II, pp. 1429, 1432-1433; *True Issue,* March 21, 1861.

center of secessionist power in Texas called for courage, but courage was not enough. As the Congressman's friend Frank Brown later wrote, Hamilton's efforts were wasted—he was only "throwing feathers against the wind."[73]

Hamilton's charge that the Secession Convention was illegal and unrepresentative of the people of Texas may have had some basis of truth. Recent studies have turned up convincing evidence of the part played by the Knights of the Golden Circle in these events. A powerful secret organization in Texas in 1860-61, the Knights were extremely influential in assembling the Secession Convention, and to a considerable extent they dominated its deliberations. There can be little doubt that this powerful organization, by agitating in favor of secession, prevented the people of the State from considering the issue calmly and objectively.[38]

Hamilton later asserted that if the true sentiments of the people of Texas could have been known, secession would have been avoided. He believed that the majority would have remained loyal to the United States. Even in the State Capitol, regardless of the attitude of most politicians, a majority of the people did not favor secession. Thus, Judge A. W. Terrell reported that every county in his judicial district, including Travis in which Austin is located, voted against the Ordinance of Secession.[39] The actual vote in Travis County was 436 for leaving the Union and 694 against. Claude Elliott, in a scholarly paper on the subject of "Union Sentiment in Texas," reached the conclusion that only one-third of the people supported the war, while one-third favored remaining in the Union, and one-third were neutral.[40]

37. Frank Brown, Annals of Travis County and the City of Austin from the Earliest Times to the Close of 1875 (n.p., n.d.), MS., typescript copy, Ch. 21, p. 22.

38. Roy Sylvan Dunn, "The KGC in Texas, 1860-1861,"*Southwestern Historical Quarterly*, LXX, pp. 558-566.

39. A. W. Terrell, "Recollections of General Sam Houston," *Texas State Historical Association Quarterly*, XIV, pp. 113-136.

40. Claude Elliott, "Union Sentiment in Texas, 1861-1865," *Southwestern Historical Quarterly*, L, pp. 449-477.

CHAPTER III

Union General and Politician

WHEN A. J. HAMILTON returned from Congress to Austin about the middle of March, 1861, the people of Texas received him with mixed emotions. The Houston *Telegraph* insisted that he had become the most unpopular man in Texas; it reported a rumor to the effect that he was so unwelcome he planned to leave the State.[1] Yet, his unpopularity could not have been prevalent throughout Texas, for he was chosen State Senator in a special election held March 25, 1861, to fill the vacancy created by the resignation of Senator R. J. Townes.[2] Editor A. B. Norton of the *Southern Intelligencer,* who gave Hamilton warm support in the race, wrote that he "has been denounced as a traitor and submissionist [but] by those for whom history will determine the proper place."[3]

Despite the considerable criticism in Austin of Hamilton and other Unionists, no real threat to his safety occurred until after the Southern reverses in the early spring of 1862. At that time the South suffered a series of critical setbacks. In Tennessee, Fort Henry and Fort Donaldson fell in February; this defeat caused the Confederates to retreat to Corinth, Mississippi, where they prepared to engage Grant's forces at Shiloh Church, another costly battle. On May 1, Federal forces captured New Orleans. The Confederates experienced a further reverse when their New Mexico Expedition failed disastrously.[4] News of these ominous events greatly excited the people of Texas, and the attitude of many toward the Union-

1. *State Gazette,* March 9, 1861 (clipping from the *Houston Telegraph*).

2. *Ibid.,* March 30, 1861.

3. *Southern Intelligencer,* March 20 and 27, 1861.

4. Samuel Eliot Morison and Henry Steele Commager, *The Growth of the American Republic* (2 vols., Oxford University Press, New York, 1950), I, p. 676; Governor Frank R. Lubbock's correspondence during the spring and early summer of 1862, Archives Division, Texas State Library.

ists stiffened. N. G. Shelly, a prominent lawyer of Austin, complained to O. M. Roberts, architect of the secession of Texas, of the traitors in their midst. Shelly intimated that some of them might well be hanged from the limbs of trees.[5]

Hamilton eventually became aware that his life was in danger, but exactly when is not clearly established. It may not have been until after the bloody Battle of Shiloh, April 5-6, 1862, and the capture of New Orleans on May 1. In a letter written almost ten years later to his daughter Mary, Hamilton recalled the death in 1862 of her young sister Katie and said that the grave had scarcely been covered before he had to flee for his life.[6]

An old rumor persists about Hamilton's escape. It is to the effect that W. W. Montgomery, whom Hamilton had successfully defended on a charge of murder, learned of a plan to seize and hang Hamilton. He warned Hamilton of the danger, then accompanied him on his flight.[7] Whether this account is true or not, it is known that Cyrus S. Mellette, staunch Unionist and friend, helped Hamilton to escape to a safe refuge in the hills west of Austin.[8] This place is located some twenty-five miles from the Capital, off Highway 71. The haven was on land once owned by Morgan C. Hamilton and named "Hamilton's Pool" for him.[9]

At the time, there was a disposition among many Southern partisans in Texas to associate A. J. Hamilton with the dissenters in the German communities and at other places in

5.   N. G. Shelley to O. M. Roberts, February 26, 1862, in O. M. Roberts' Letters, IV, MS. 8216, Archives, University of Texas Library.

6.   A. J. Hamilton to Mary Hamilton Mills, September 15, 1871, in A. J. Hamilton Papers, Archives, University of Texas Library. Katie Hamilton's gravestone shows only 1858-1862, and the Oakwood Cemetery records show only 1862.

7.   Nannie M. Tilley (ed.), *Federals on the Frontier: The Diary of Benjamin F. McIntyre* (University of Texas Press, Austin, 1963), p. 318; Miss Tilley's comments in the footnote on same page.

8.   Interview of Pauline A. Pinkney, granddaughter of C. S. Mellette, by John L. Waller, February 13, 1962.

9.   Frank Brown, Annals of Travis County and the City of Austin from the Earliest Times to the Close of 1875, Ch. 17, pp. 1-74, MS., typescript copy, n. p., n. d., Archives, University of Texas Library; Interview of John H. Chiles, great grandson of A. J. Hamilton, by John L. Waller, October 8, 1963.

the State. From Bandera, in the hill country west of Austin, came a report that a document had been discovered on which appeared Hamilton's signature, proving his association with the Unionists.[10] Rumors spread that Hamilton had recruited a strong force of Germans near Austin to oppose secession— an offense that, if true, would have called for severe punishment.[11]

Aware of charges of this kind and of the danger they entailed, Hamilton, some time in July, 1862, along with a group of friends left the refuge on horseback for Mexico. Toward the end of the month, he and fifteen others reached Matamoros. The American consul at Matamoros, Leonard Pierce, reported to Secretary of State Seward the arrival of Hamilton and his party. The consul also told of seeing Hamilton and a few others safely aboard an American vessel, the *U.S.S. Sperry,* bound for the port of New Orleans, now in Union hands.[12] A later report indicated that a plot to capture Hamilton had been discovered, and that Consul Pierce was so uneasy that he had sent Hamilton and a few others by night to the mouth of the Rio Grande to board the ship. The excitement was so great that the vessel hurriedly put to sea, leaving behind its chief officer and clearance orders.[13]

The trip to New Orleans was made safely. Some time after his arrival, Hamilton, on September 27, made an emotional speech in Lyceum Hall before the Loyal League of the city. He thanked God for once again being able to enjoy freedom of speech; he denied that secession was really approved by the people of Texas; he designated ministers who preached secession as "reverend cutthroats"; he criticised the treachery of General David E. Twiggs for surrendering the army

10. *State Gazette,* June 1, 1861.
11. *War of Rebellion: Official Records of the Union and Confederate Armies* (130 vols., Washington, D. C., 1880-1901), Ser. I, Vol. IX, p. 684. (Hereinafter cited as *O. R.*)
12. Consul Leonard Pierce, Jr., to Secretary of State Seward, August 26, 1862, in Consular Dispatches, Matamoros, Mexico, Microfilm, vol. VII, roll II, Garcia Collection, University of Texas Library.
13. M. W. Lamb to Secretary of State Seward, November 2, 1862, in Consular Dispatches, Matamoros, Microfilm, vol. VII.

post and munitions of war at San Antonio even before secession was proclaimed. Hamilton also claimed that after he had
fled, a military squad had entered his home and told his wife
that if her husband had been there he would have been hanged in her presence from one of his own shade trees. The
speech closed with a strong appeal for loyalty to the Union
and an expression of love for and devotion to its flag.[14]

During his address, Hamilton urged the loyal group at
New Orleans to raise funds for aiding others who might
arrive empty handed. It is likely that he was short of funds
himself. An unfriendly observer wrote that Hamilton was in
desperate circumstances. According to this account, although
the fleeing Texan had obtained some cash from Santiago
Vidaurri, Governor of the Mexican States of Coahuila and
Nuevo León, he had squandered it: upon reading a newspaper report that General George B. McClellan had captured
Richmond, Hamilton had gone on a "big bust" and spent
his last cent.[15] There may have been some truth in this statement. Hamilton did maintain some relations with Governor
Vidaurri, as will appear later, and he was known to drink
rather freely when under emotional stress.

A reporter for the New York *Tribune* who heard Hamilton's address concluded an account of it with "We hope to
hear him again." The same issue of the newspaper contained
a statement insisting that Hamilton should be heard in New
York City, where no part of the country was so little known
as Texas.[16] The thought was father to the act. On October 2,
the *Tribune* announced that Hamilton would deliver two
speeches in New York, one that evening in the Brooklyn Academy of Music, and the other two nights later at the Cooper
Union Institute.

The *Tribune* of October 3 contained a report of Hamilton's
first speech. The report indicated that his argument was based
on the conspiracy theory: that the slave-holding aristocracy

14. New York *Tribune*, September 29, 1862.
15. *State Gazette*, August 20, 1862 (clipping from San Antonio Herald); New
York *Tribune*, October 10, 1862 (clipping from Grenada *Appeal*).
16. New York *Tribune*, September 29, 1862.

of the South deliberately planned to strengthen its grip on the region by making slavery permanent. In the course of his remarks, Hamilton said that he had owned a few slaves, but, having concluded that secession, if successful, would end democracy and stultify laboring white men, he had determined to give all possible support to the cause of preserving the Union.

On October 4, the editorial comment in the *Tribune* praised Hamilton's oratory, which, it remarked, convinced every hearer that there was a "death-grapple between slavery and freedom, aristocracy and democracy; that all talk of conciliation is twaddle, and that the only peace possible must be found by the bayonet."[17]

In the addresses in New York, Hamilton made it clear that he was heartily in sympathy with Lincoln's Preliminary Emancipation Proclamation, issued September 22, 1862. When rumors began to circulate that the spirit of the proclamation might be weakened or compromised, Hamilton wrote the President a long and eloquent letter, urging him to resist any modification. Hamilton pointed out that in promising freedom to the slaves, the proclamation had won the friendship of European humanitarians opposed to slavery. They had been able to block the intervention of England and France in the war. Hamilton finally reminded the President that he had invoked God's blessing on the proclamation, and that its high spirit and purpose should remain undisturbed.[18]

While in New Orleans, Hamilton had talked with George S. Denison, who had lived for several years in San Antonio, Texas, in the 1850's. Knowing of Hamilton's unionism, Denison had given him a letter of introduction to his kinsman Secretary of the Treasury Salmon P. Chase.[19] Hamilton took the opportunity made possible by his trip north to call

17. *Ibid.*, October 2, 3, 4, 1862.
18. John L. Haynes to Mrs. W.W. Mills, July 10, 1875, in A. J. Hamilton Papers, Archives, University of Texas Library.
19. Edward G. Bourne, et al. (eds.), "Diary and Correspondence of S. P. Chase," *Annual Report of the American Historical Association for the Year 1902*, II, pp. 314-315.

on the Secretary in Washington. An entry in Chase's diary of October 5, 1862, notes that A. J. Hamilton dined with him and friends and talked of his escape from Texas and of the distressing conditions in the State. In the course of their discussion, Hamilton declared that an oligarchy wanted to retain slavery and lord it over the less affluent whites. Chase endorsed Hamilton's estimate of the situation and promised to arrange for him a meeting with President Lincoln.[20] Chase's diary entry for October 6 indicates that the meeting with the President was arranged, but it does not give the date.[21]

On October 10, Chase recorded a conversation in which he proposed that Hamilton go to Ohio and make a number of speeches. It is likely that Hamilton made this trip; after the war he would be invited to speak in Ohio during the congressional campaign of 1866.[22] The meeting with Lincoln must have occurred soon after Hamilton's initial contact with Chase, for on November 14, 1862, Hamilton was commissioned Brigadier General of Volunteers and Military Governor of Texas.[23] It is unlikely that Lincoln would have approved this important appointment without having interviewed and measured the competence of the man selected.

In his interviews with President Lincoln and other high officials of the National Government, Hamilton doubtless stressed his belief that the sentiment of loyalty was widespread in Western Texas. He probably suggested that many Texans, if given the opportunity, would enlist in the Federal Army. Hamilton's appointment may have been partly for the purpose of enlisting the loyal Texans who had escaped to Mexico. Denison, in his letter to Chase, suggested that Hamilton be encouraged to enlist a brigade of West Texas Unionists.

On at least one occasion, Hamilton requested, without success, that Union troopships be used to take Texas refugees

20. *Ibid.*, p. 101. 21. *Ibid.*, p. 102.
22. *Ibid.*, p. 104; C. Delano and three other Congressmen, July 16, 1866, Petition to A. J. Hamilton, in A. J. Hamilton papers, Archives, University of Texas Library.
23. Records of the Adjutant General's Office, H 1263, Commission Branch, 1862, National Archives, Washington, D.C.; *O. R.*, Ser. III, Vol. II, pp. 782-783.

from the Rio Grande to New Orleans.[24] Texans did enlist in the Federal forces. Two regiments, the First and Second Texas Cavalry, were raised by E. J. Davis, John L. Haynes, and others. These troops rendered effective service during the Federal occupation of the Gulf Coast and the Rio Grande during the late fall of 1863 and early spring of 1864.[25]

Though twice given the commission of Brigadier General of Volunteers, Hamilton took no part in military activities. He realized that the best contribution he could make to the Union cause would derive from his oratorical talents and political skills. It is true that he maintained headquarters in New Orleans, and that a regular staff and a small military detachment were assigned to him.[26] However, Secretary of War Stanton made it clear in a letter of November 14, 1862, addressed to Hamilton—a letter accompanying his commission—that his special duty as Military Governor of Texas would be to reestablish the Federal Government in Texas. General N. P. Banks, Union commander in the area, was ordered to cooperate with Hamilton and to supply him, upon request, with sufficient military forces to uphold his authority.[27]

Hamilton's commission as Brigadier General seems to have been fully justified—this because his political function proved significant. Hamilton was quite influential in creating a demand in the North and East for the invasion of Texas, and in building and sustaining morale in those areas. Texans followed his activities with considerable interest. Not many forgot or forgave him, though he was far away from the State.[28]

24. *O. R.*, Ser. I, Vol. XV, p. 658; Edward G. Bourne, et al. (eds.), "Diary and Correspondence of S. P. Chase," II, pp. 314-315.
25. Frank Herbert Smyrl, "Unionism, Abolitionism, Vigilantism" (M. A. thesis, University of Texas, 1961), pp. 146-149, 160; *O. R.*, Ser. I, XLI, p. 186.
26. Records of the Adjutant General's Office, H 1263, Commission Branch; *ibid.*, H 842, for 1863, National Archives; Sgt. Adam Forbes to General A. J. Hamilton, November 25, 1864, in A. J. Hamilton Papers, Archives, University of Texas Library.
27. *O. R.*, Ser. II, Vol. III, pp. 782-783; *ibid.*, Ser. I, Vol. XXVI, Pt. I, p. 902; Records of the Adjutant General's Office, Record Group 94, H 1262 and 1263, Commission Branch, National Archives.
28. Houston *Telegraph*, March 27, 1863.

Meanwhile, by the middle of 1862, the excitement in Texas over secession that had characterized the early phases of volunteering began to wane. In the sections of the State where the vote against secession had been strong—as in North Texas along the Red River and in the German communities—deep suspicions arose among the protagonists of the Southern cause. As extensive membership in Union associations was revealed, fears mounted; many men were arrested, and frightful punishments were meted out.

Irregular courts, such as the "Citizens' Council" in Gainesville, Cooke County, Texas, denied to the accused the safeguards guaranteed by the State Constitution, such as grand jury indictment, habeas corpus, defense counsel, and the unanimous agreement of a legally constituted jury for the sentence of death.[29] Governor Francis R. Lubbock, though apparently approving the procedures at Gainesville, characterized them as a "terrible and speedy, *though unauthorized* [his emphasis], vengeance on the traitors."[30] The proceedings at Gainesville would almost surely have been repeated at Sherman in Grayson County, where a large group of suspects had been seized, had it not been for the courageous and eloquent appeal made by James Webb Throckmorton, subsequently Governor of Texas.[31] This violent action of the pro-slavery partisans won no support for the Confederacy. General Henry E. McCulloch, Confederate commander in the area, estimated a year after these events that there were a thousand deserters and draft-dodgers in his district.[32]

Hamilton, of course, was acquainted with the nature and

29. Thomas Barrett, *The Great Hanging at Gainesville, Cooke County, Texas, A.D. 1862* (Gainesville, Texas, 1885; State Historical Association, Austin, 1961), *passim*; Sam Acheson and Julie Ann Hudson O'Connell (eds.), "George Washington Diamond's Account of the Great Hanging at Gainesville, 1862," *Southwestern Historical Quarterly*, LXVI, pp. 331-414.

30. Governor Lubbock to Confederate Senator L. T. Wigfall, October 27, 1862, in Executive Record Book, No. 281, pp. 393-395, Archives Division, Texas State Library.

31. J. W. Throckmorton to J. J. Diamond, May 25, 1867, in J. W. Throckmorton Correspondence, A 17/59, Archives, University of Texas Library.

32. Brigadier General H. E. McCulloch to General J. Bankhead Magruder, October 21, 1863, in *O. R.*, Ser. I, Vol. XXVI, Pt. II, pp. 325-327.

extent of the dissension in Texas. Therefore, seeing an opportunity to advance the interests of the Union, he urged upon Chase, Stanton, Seward, and Lincoln the importance of an invasion of Texas. All of these leaders were in sympathy with the idea but they were obliged to support military activities in more vital areas.

In addition to seeking the aid of those who decided policy in Washington, Hamilton appealed to the political and business leaders of the North to support his proposal of invasion. He emphasized to them the importance of access to the cotton market of the State, noting that even after the Federal forces had captured New Orleans on May 1, 1862, the movement of cotton to the North had not met its needs.[33] The influential New York *Times* in its issue of October 23, 1862, came out strongly in favor of winning control of Texas, where, the newspaper asserted, more cotton could be raised with free labor than had been produced previously by the entire South with 4,000,000 slaves.

Arguments such as these, however, did not prevail. The policy makers in Washington insisted that a grand strategy of the war must be formulated and sustained. The so-called Anaconda Policy proposed by General Winfield Scott called for the mastery of the Mississippi River, as well as the division of the Southern Confederacy and the defeat of each part of it in turn. This approach became increasingly important after the fighting before Richmond had developed into something of a stalemate. Even while Hamilton was making his appeals in New York and New England for an invasion of Texas, Lincoln was deciding to concentrate on the capture of Vicksburg and Port Hudson in order to gain control of the Father of Waters.

In preparation for an invasion of Texas, a special force of some 15,000 men was raised and placed under the command of General N. P. Banks, an influential New England

33. A. J. Hamilton's correspondence with prominent men in New York and New England during fall of 1862 and spring of 1863, in A. J. Hamilton Papers, Archives, University of Texas Library.

politician.[34] General Banks invited Hamilton and his staff to join the force, but he later stated that a nondescript group of speculators forced their way on board the troopships. Banks, however, wrote more kindly when corresponding with Lincoln; moreover, the General, in making his final report, showed high respect for Hamilton.[35]

To further the main objective of winning control of the Mississippi River, John A. McClernand, former congressional colleague of Hamilton, raised a large number of troops in the Northwest, which were added to the armies being assembled. We shall hear more of McClernand and his association with Hamilton in the activities along the Rio Grande. To General U.S. Grant was assigned the overall command of the campaign to capture Vicksburg and Port Hudson, last Confederate defenses on the Mississippi. This assignment was all-important. To add to Grant's effectiveness, Lincoln, without informing the public or the New England governors, decided that Banks should cooperate with Grant, commander of the Federal forces in the West.[36]

What was Hamilton's role under Banks? He had two commissions: Brigadier General of Volunteers and Military Governor of Texas. In neither of these capacities did he exercise command over any of the forces assigned to Banks. Since the initial objective of these forces had been changed from invading Texas to taking control of the Mississippi, one may ask why Hamilton was taken along, especially since his commission as brigadier general was soon revoked, or allowed to lapse.[37] Banks did not inform Hamilton of the change in their objective until after they had entered the Mississippi River.

34. Ludwell H. Johnson, *The Red River Campaign: Politics and Cotton in the Civil War* (Johns Hopkins Press, Baltimore, c. 1958), pp. 9-13, 20-24; *Dictionary of American Biography* (20 vols., Charles Scribner's Sons, New York, 1943-_____), I, p. 579.

35. *O. R.,* Ser. I, Vol. XV, pp. 200-201; *ibid.,* Ser. I, Vol. XXVI, Pt. I, pp. 6-7.

36. Lord Charwood, *Abraham Lincoln* (Garden City Publishing Co., Garden City, New York, 1917), pp. 339, 349-355; *O. R.,* Ser. I, Vol. XV, pp. 296-300.

37. Records of the Adjutant General's Office, H 1263, Commission Branch, 1862; *ibid.,* 1863, National Archives; Ludwell H. Johnson, *op. cit.,* pp. 14-24; *O. R.,* Ser. I, Vol. XV, pp. 200, 642, 656.

Hamilton protested strongly. Banks, so he said later, in order to appease Hamilton ordered an attack on Galveston, Texas.

By now, the Confederate forces had all but abandoned the defense of Galveston. On October 4, 1862, Colonel Isaac Burrell, with some 260 Massachusetts troops, established a foothold on the wharfs. He expected reinforcements; Banks had ample time to send them, but he did not act. As a result, the Confederates under General J. Bankhead Magruder re-captured Galveston on January 1, 1863.[38] General Banks later explained his action, or inaction, to the Secretary of War; in making his final report, he frankly confessed that the greatest error of his entire campaign was his failure to establish a firm grip on Galveston Island.[39]

When Hamilton became convinced that the detachment at Galveston was not to be strengthened, he returned to the North, hoping to organize another Texas expedition. In this mission, he received strong support. Thus, Governor J. A. Gilmore of New Hampshire wrote President Lincoln in mid-August, 1863, requesting the reappointment of Hamilton to his military position and giving assurances that the necessary troops would be raised. Other New England governors rein-forced this endorsement.[40] On August 20, Secretary of the Treasury Chase wrote Hamilton a letter of encouragement concerning the redemption of Texas, and expressing great confidence in him. President Lincoln personally approved this letter.[41] That appeals in Hamilton's behalf were effective is indicated by his receiving a new commission as Brigadier General of Volunteers (dated September 18, 1863, which he accepted on September 22).[42]

Hamilton had all along been making speeches in different

38. *Ibid.*, Ser. I, Vol. IX, pp. 709-713; *ibid.*, Ser. I, Vol. XV, pp. 150, 868.
39. General Banks to Chief of Staff H. W. Halleck, January 7, 1863, in *O. R.* Ser. I, Vol. XV, p. 200; *ibid.*, Ser. I, Vol. XXVI, p. 6.
40. *Ibid.*, Ser. I, Vol. XV, pp. 680, 832.
41. Secretary of the United States Treasury S. P. Chase to A. J. Hamilton, August 20, 1863 (with President Lincoln's endorsement), in A. J. Hamilton Papers, Archives, University of Texas Library.
42. Records of the Adjutant General's Office, Commission Branch, H 842, and Commission Branch, H 407 (H 1105), 1863, National Archives.

parts of the North and East. He was able to revive interest in the Texas campaign, especially since the first army of Banks had been assigned to aid Grant in reducing Vicksburg and Port Hudson to Federal control. On September 27, 1862, Hamilton had delivered a speech in New Orleans which was reported by the New York *Tribune* correspondent and published October 2 with strong editorial support. Soon thereafter, Hamilton had been invited to speak in Brooklyn and New York City, as well as in other places in the State.[43] As a result, he had won a host of enthusiastic friends in New York, among whom was John Austin Stevens, Jr., influential official in the New York City Chamber of Commerce. A number of letters from Stevens to Hamilton indicated a continuing interest in the Texas expedition and serious efforts on the part of the writer to bring it about. Other prominent men in the city such as James Wadsworth, Mayor George Opdyke, and Hiram Walbridge—gave the aggressive Texan much encouragement.

The New York press, however else it might differ, united in praising Hamilton's oratorical efforts. He soon had calls from New England—from influential men like Edward Atkinson, textile manufacturer and author of Brookline, Massachusetts; Alexander H. Rice, member of the Thirty-sixth Congress, from Massachusetts; James G. Blaine, and the governors of the New England states.[44] The Colt's Manufacturing Company of Hartford, Connecticut, must have regarded Hamilton as an important and influential person, for on April 22, 1863, they sent him a repeating shotgun, "as a slight token of our friendship."[45] He was invited to speak at several places throughout New England, and he received urgent calls for return engagements.

Back in Texas, A. J. Hamilton enjoyed far less popularity. Editor Cushing of the Houston *Telegraph* published the story that Hamilton had been unable to obtain a hall in Boston

43. New York *Tribune,* September 29, October 2, 3, 4, 1862.
44. A. J. Hamilton Papers, Archives, University of Texas Library.
45 *Ibid.*

for an address. The editor added that the traitor had at last sunk to the lowest level by being spurned by those to whom he had fled.[46] The facts are that Hamilton spoke in both Faneuil Hall and Tremont Temple—and he impressed some listeners so much that they considered him a worthy successor, as an orator, to the mighty Webster. The pledges of the governors of the North to assist Hamilton in raising troops for the occupation of Texas did not fall on deaf ears in Washington, as will be made clear in the following chapter.[47]

Meanwhile, as Hamilton continued making his appeals, General Banks began a campaign, during the spring of 1863, which led into the Teche region of Central Louisiana. Here he encountered little opposition, and his movement soon developed into a gigantic raid and pillaging expedition. Forgetting that his assignment was to cooperate with Grant in capturing Vicksburg and Port Hudson, Banks began to think in grandiose terms. He concluded that he could overrun all of northern and western Louisiana, occupy Shreveport, and invade Texas, *if* only Grant would cooperate with him. He therefore suggested that Grant send some 20,000 troops, including Benjamin H. Grierson's cavalry—an instance, as it were, of the tail trying to wag the dog.

When Grant declined and reminded Banks of the main objectives, the rebuffed leader somewhat reluctantly lowered his sights. Even so, he did insist on salvaging the enormous quantities of cotton and other supplies that he had taken. After seeing them safely on the way to New Orleans, General Banks proceeded to lay siege to Port Hudson. As a result of Grant's driving force, Vicksburg fell on July 4, and Port Hudson five days later.[48] The way now seemed open for a second attempt to invade Texas.

46. Houston *Telegraph,* July 10, 1863.

47. Resolution of thanks, April 18, 1863, for address delivered in Faneuil Hall, Boston, in A. J. Hamilton Papers, Archives, University of Texas Library.

48. *O. R.,* Ser. I, Vol. XV, pp. 296, 309, 314, 671, 706, 728; *ibid.,* Ser. I, Vol. XXVI, Pt. I, pp. 499, 564, 574, 624, 659.

CHAPTER IV

Hamilton and the Invasion of Texas

SHORTLY AFTER the Union forces had won control of the Mississippi River, President Abraham Lincoln wrote General N. P. Banks of his hope that the flag would be planted in Texas and that Hamilton would be established as Military Governor of the State. Lincoln indicated his confidence in Hamilton as a man of worth and ability, and expressed concern for the plight of his family. In substance, Banks replied that he would be pleased to cooperate with Hamilton.[1]

It is likely that Hamilton accompanied reinforcements sent to Banks in New Orleans in the summer of 1863, for he was in this city by early fall. A friend of his, S. M. Swenson, had left Austin early in October and had reached Matamoros, Mexico, on October 30. Swenson wrote his wife of receiving news from New Orleans that General Hamilton had arrived from New York on October 14, "temperate in habits and sober-minded," and that he was reported to be in strong favor with President Lincoln.[2]

At this time, General U.S. Grant—and General Banks at first—favored concentration of the assault on Mobile. A number of factors, however, tipped the scales in support of a move toward Texas. There was resentment in New England over the failure to use the troops recruited in the area for the earlier invasion of Texas. The Maximilian Expedition into Mexico, conceived by Emperor Louis Napoleon and supported by French troops, emphasized the need for American forces in the border area. The plight of the Unionists in Texas appealed to Lincoln; he agreed that military measures should be taken

1. Roy Basler (ed.), *The Collected Works of Abraham Lincoln* (8 vols., Springfield, Illinois, 1953), VI, p. 465.
2. S. M. Swenson to his wife, November 3, 1863, in S. M. Swenson Papers, Archives, University of Texas Library.

in their behalf. The big question now was, what route should an invasion follow?

Banks, who apparently had considerable freedom of action, decided to enter Texas first via Sabine Pass. The expedition was placed under the command of General William B. Franklin, but it proved ill-fated. Poor navigation caused one of the Union ships to run aground and tilt in such a way that it could not bring its guns to bear on the fort. A lucky shot from the Confederate fort struck a vital part of another ship. This reverse was enough to discourage the faint-hearted Franklin, even though he commanded a large body of troops. If he had only wanted to do so, he could have landed a small detachment and outflanked the fort.

As it was, the plucky defender, Lieutenant Dick Dowling, the Texas commander, had only a squad of men and six small cannon. With these, he held off—bluffed off—the Union general's potentially more powerful forces.[3] Colonel A. J. H. Duganne, a Union prisoner in Camp Ford near Tyler, Texas, wrote a devastating criticism of the repulse. He termed it a disgraceful defeat, "which should have been punished by a proper court-martial." Although the reports in the New York papers described Franklin's failure "as a gallant struggle with overwhelming odds," Duganne concluded that "the facts were the American squadron and army . . . had retreated from the coast . . . shamefully driven off by forty-two Irish militiamen in a mud hut with six pieces of artillery."[4]

Next, after considerable uncertainty and delay, the Union strategists chose the Red River route for the main invasion. Preceding this move, however, General Banks sent an expedition to the mouth of the Rio Grande. It landed successfully, November 2, 1863, at Brazos Santiago, the pass commanding the entrance to the river at the southern tip of Texas. Sub-

3. Alwyn Barr, "Texas Coastal Defenses, 1861-1865," *Southwestern Historical Quarterly*, LXV, pp. 23-27; W. P. Ballinger, Diary, entry of September 14, 1863, Archives, University of Texas Library.

4. A. J. H. Duganne, *Camps and Prisons: Twenty Months in the Department of the Gulf* (3rd edition, J. P. Robens, New York, 1865), p. 258.

sequently, the Union forces occupied the territory along the river as far as Roma, and along the Gulf Coast as far as Aransas Pass. Why the Federal occupation was not extended eastward along the coast to Galveston, or inland to San Antonio, has never been fully explained. To General Banks, however, it was clear that a much larger force than the one available at the time would have been required to occupy the coast from Brazos Santiago to Galveston, or to take and hold San Antonio. If the objective of the Rio Grande Expedition had been accomplished, the cotton trade through Mexico, almost vital to keeping Texas and the Trans-Mississippi Department of the Confederacy in the war, would have been closed.[5]

Because of its enormous cotton production and its proximity to the Rio Grande, Texas was all-important to the Confederacy.[6] In order to increase contributions of the State to the Southern cause, Governor Francis R. Lubbock persuaded the Legislature to create the Texas State Military Board. It was authorized to buy and sell cotton, build ammunition factories, and engage in any other activities that might advance the war effort.[7] The records of the Board are in such confusion that it is possible only approximately to ascertain the volume of its business.[8] Nevertheless, one thing is certain: As a result of its decisions, thousands of bales of cotton produced in Texas, and on farms and plantations as far away as Arkansas and Louisiana, were laboriously hauled

5. *War of Rebellion: Official Records of the Union and Confederate Armies* (130 vols., Washington, D. C., 1880-1901), Ser. I, Vol. XXVI, Pt. I, pp. 856, 678. (Hereinafter cited as O. R.)

6. Annie Cowling, "The Civil War Trade of the Lower Rio Grande Valley" (M. A. thesis, University of Texas, 1926), *passim;* Leroy P. Graf, *The Economic History of the Lower Rio Grande Valley, 1820-1875* (Cambridge, Massachusetts), typescript copy in Eugene Campbell Barker Texas History Center, University of Texas Library), I, pp. 489-514.

7. H. P. N. Gammel (comp.), *Laws of Texas* (10 vols., Austin, 1898), V, pp. 484, 489.

8. E. M. Pease-Swante Palm Report, in Executive Record Book, No. 281, pp. 94-119; Executive Record Book, No. 81, pp. 124-128, 155-157, 318-333, both in Archives Division, Texas State Library.

across the wide expanses of Texas to Mexico, and millions of dollars worth of materials were brought back in exchange.[9]

Yet, this trade in cotton and war supplies entailed certain disadvantages. So much suspicion resulted from the activities of those who engaged in it that it tended to weaken the morale of the people of Texas. They became increasingly critical of all persons believed to be profiting from the business. Even Governor Lubbock and his successor, Governor Murrah, as well as General Magruder, became suspect.[10]

Hamilton did not accompany the Rio Grande Expedition that occupied Brazos Santiago. Banks felt that if the expedition failed, Hamilton's presence would magnify the setback; otherwise any reverse might be explained away as an unsuccessful raid. This was sound reasoning, and Hamilton agreed with it.[11] As soon as a landing was secured at Brazos Santiago, Hamilton went to Brownsville, Texas, located nearby, where he promptly began to function as Military Governor. Shortly after arriving in Brownsville, he issued a "Proclamation to the People of Texas,"[12] which was in effect an appeal to the slaves freed by Emancipation and to the nonslaveholding whites. Although Hamilton's proclamation aroused the opposition of certain editors, it is doubtful if any appreciable number of Texans read it—or even heard of it.[13] In issuing

9. J. B. Earle to W. P. Ballinger, March 19, 1864, in W. P. Ballinger Papers, Archives, University of Texas Library; William Diamond, "Imports of the Confederate Government from Europe and Mexico," *Journal of Southern History,* VI, pp. 470-503; Ralph W. Delaney, "Port for Texas During the Civil War," *Southwestern Historical Quarterly,* LVIII, pp. 473-487; *State Gazette,* April 1, 8, 15, 1863; Houston *Telegraph,* May 1, July 3, 1863; *True Issue,* December 10, 1864 (clipping from *Gonzalez Inquirer,* Gonzalez, Texas).

10. Houston *Telegraph,* May 23, July 3, 1863; Ralph W. Delaney, "Ports for Texas During the Civil War," *op. cit.;* Mrs. Sara Wharton to W. P. Ballinger, October 23, 1863; Thomas F. McKinney to W. P. Ballinger, October 4, 1864—W. P. Ballinger Papers, Archives, University of Texas Library.

11. A. J. Hamilton to Secretary of War E. M. Stanton, December 19, 1863, in Correspondence of the War Department, H. 123/124, Box 301, National Archives.

12. Rough draft of Proclamation; also "An Address to the People of Texas," New Orleans, April 2, 1865—both in A. J. Hamilton Papers, Archives, University of Texas Library.

13. Houston *Tri-Weekly Telegraph,* February 15, March 4, 1864; *Tri-Weekly State Gazette,* February 15, 1864.

the statement, Hamilton hoped to weaken the morale of those who supported the war. He sternly warned them of the suffering, such as burdensome taxation and military oppression, that they would surely experience if they continued on their present course.

Acting in his capacity of Military Governor, even before coming to Texas, Hamilton began making appointments. One of his first official acts was to name Isaac B. McFarland as district judge of the newly established civil court. In addition, Hamilton made these appointments: Ezekiel B. Turner, prosecuting attorney; A. C. Buddington, clerk of the court; Seth B. Reid, marshal of the court; Joseph W. Talbott, brigadier general of the militia of the district; Josiah Moorhead, auctioneer and notary public in Brownsville; Hezekiah B. Hamilton, wreck-master of Cameron County; and Henry Applegate, detective.[14]

Meanwhile, Hamilton had received news that proved shocking to him for personal reasons. He had learned of the kidnapping and murder of his friend W. W. Montgomery—the man who reportedly had earlier accompanied him on his flight from Austin. Montgomery had later gone from New Orleans to Matamoros with Colonel E. J. Davis to bring the Davis family to New Orleans. When Colonel George W. Chilton, a Confederate officer stationed at Brownsville, learned that this Union detachment had crossed the Rio Grande, he led a group of men in pursuit, capturing Davis, Montgomery, and a few others. These were promptly escorted back to Texas; and Montgomery, along with several other men, were summarily hung.

Detective Applegate, investigating the hanging, located one of the suspected participants in Matamoros—a man named Dick Hamilton, no relation to the Governor. After the Mexicans had delivered the suspect to A. J. Hamilton at his request, he turned the prisioner over to Major General N. J. T. Dana, subordinate Union commander in Texas, expecting him to arrange a military trial. Dana, however, objected

14. Election Register, No. 260, p. 4, Archives Division, Texas State Library.

to this procedure; in doing so, he received the backing not only of his superior, General N. P. Banks, but also of Secretaries Stanton and Seward in Washington. Under these circumstances, Hamilton was obliged to postpone his efforts to bring the killers of Montgomery to justice. But sometime later, after he had become Provisional Governor, Hamilton again turned his attention to the crime, instructing the district judges and district attorneys whom he had appointed in the Brownsville area to collect evidence on which to base a prosecution. As a result, on May 19, 1866, the grand jury of the Twelfth Judicial District returned an indictment against G. W. Chilton and others "for the murder by hanging of W. W. Montgomery." The case, however, never came to trial, owing principally to the confusion that prevailed during the Reconstruction Period.[15]

While serving at Brownsville, Governor Hamilton delivered several speeches. On March 22, 1864, he addressed the First Texas Cavalry Regiment, Colonel E. J. Davis commanding.[16] Nine days later, he responded to a petition of old friends by delivering an address on "The Great Issues Involved in the Contest now Being Waged for the Maintenance of Liberty and the Integrity of our Government." Among those present were F. B. Coupland, E. J. Davis, W. P. DeNormandie, Federal Judge Thomas H. Duval, G. D. Kingsbury, Judge I. B. McFarland, Alex. Rossy, Jesse Stancel, and E. B. Turner.[17]

For another speech during his stay in Brownsville, Governor Hamilton received an implied censure. His remarks were made at a sumptuous dinner given for him and General John A. McClernand, his former congressional colleague. The banquet was held across the Rio Grande in Matamoros, with

15. O. R., Ser. I, Vol. XXVI, Pt. I, pp. 842, 856-859; ibid., Ser. I, pp. 1013, 1128; District Court Records, Twelfth Judicial District, Brownsville, Texas, April 23, 1866, pp. 275, 319 (courtesy of Mark Sherrill).

16. Nannie M. Tilley (ed.), Federals on the Frontier: The Diary of Benjamin F. McIntyre (University of Texas, Austin, 1963), p. 315. (Cited hereinafter as McIntyre's Diary.) G. D. Kingsbury Papers, Archives, University of Texas.

17. Ibid.; McIntyre's Diary, p. 318.

General Juan Cortinas, Mexican military commander, serving as host. According to the New Orleans *Picayune,* which based its account on one published in *El Zaragoza,* a newspaper supporting Benito Juárez, the occasion was a "Banquet and Ball" at which many toasts and speeches were delivered. In responding to one of the toasts, Hamilton was reported to have spoken eloquently and frankly, expressing the hope that the French should be driven out of Mexico.[18]

Someone unfriendly to Hamilton, or an agent of the State Department, sent the *Picayune* article to Seward, Secretary of State in Washington. He notified Hamilton that he had received the article and suggested that the Governor might wish to give an explanation of his purported remarks. Secretary of War Stanton endorsed the letter, thus making it an order that called for a response. Hamilton meanwhile had gone to New Orleans, from which point on June 15, 1864, he mailed an official reply to the inquiry. He explained that he had proposed a toast to Benito Juárez, the Mexican revolutionary leader, in reply to a toast given in honor of Abraham Lincoln, the American war leader, on the theme of preserving Republican institutions.[19]

Evidently the answer to the demand for an explanation was satisfactory to Hamilton's superiors for they did not revoke his commissions. In point of fact, it may be assumed that under the mellowing influence of good food, good fellowship, and good wine, the Governor had waxed overly eloquent and sympathetic. He probably did not stop to think of the diplomatic faux pas he was committing.

Before the Federal forces could occupy the lower Rio Grande valley and the Gulf Coast, the Union military leaders decided to invade Texas by another route: by way of the Red River. In the early spring of 1864, the strategists in Washington speeded up their preparations for the invasion.

18. *Ibid.,* p. 325; *Picayune (New Orleans),* February 9, April 27, 1864.

19. Letter, May 9, 1864, from State Department of the United States to Military Governor A. J. Hamilton, and his reply of June 15, 1864, in A. J. Hamilton Papers, Archives, University of Texas Library.

They ordered all troops stationed in Texas, except a token force left at Brazos Santiago, back to Louisiana in support of the Red River expedition. General McClernand was recalled from a special assignment as commander of Federal forces in Texas to lead the Thirteenth Army Corps in Louisiana.[20] The 1st and 2nd Texas Cavalry regiments, under the command respectively of Colonels E. J. Davis and John L. Haynes, were sent to New Orleans late in May.[21] Governor Hamilton, with General F. J. Herron, had left on May 6 for New Orleans.[22]

The Red River expedition, now assembled, was placed under the command of General Banks. But before reaching Shreveport, Louisiana, three-quarters of the distance upriver to Texas, it was halted; it then turned back to the Mississippi River. As for Hamilton: whatever may have been his military duties after he returned to New Orleans, he seems to have been relieved of them. By the end of the fall of 1864, "General Hamilton's Guard" was assigned to duties elsewhere, much to the unhappiness of the men who comprised it.[23]

Yet, Hamilton retained his military commissions. The explanation lies in the political service he was able to render Lincoln and the Union Party in the presidential election of 1864. Although the convention of the Republican Party, joined by Unionist Democrats, had renominated Lincoln, he faced strong opposition in the election campaign. The abolitionist Republicans had chosen John C. Fremont as their candidate, and the Democrats had nominated General George B. McClellan. Lincoln's running mate was Andrew Johnson, Unionist Democrat.[24] New York was a crucial State in the election, and the Lincoln forces enlisted Hamilton's support, knowing of his popularity in the area. He forthwith undertook a speak-

20. *Picayune,* May 5, 1864.
21. New York *Tribune,* June 1, 1864.   22. *Ibid.,* May 31, 1864.
23. Sergt. Adams Forbes to General A. J. Hamilton, November 25, 1864, in A. J. Hamilton Papers, Archives, University of Texas Library.
24. Samuel Eliot Morison and Henry Steele Commager, *The Growth of the American Republic* (2 vols., Oxford University Press, New York, 1950), I, pp. 622, 624, 731.

ing tour for Lincoln and the Union Party. Opening the series of appearances at Cooper Union Institute on October 14, he was greeted with "tempestuous applause." This speech was followed by others at diverse points: Albion, Medina, Batavia, Brockport, Genesee, Penn-Yan, Palmyra, Lyons, Mayville, Ithaca, and Albany. He concluded his tour at Troy on November 7, the day before the election.[25]

Hamilton arrived back in New Orleans on November 19. On the 29th he addressed a large meeting there, held to celebrate the reelection of Lincoln, at which William P. Fessenden, Secretary of the United States Treasury, spoke. Hamilton was "well received" by the audience.[26]

President Lincoln had earlier expressed his appreciation of Hamilton's support by issuing him a special permit for moving cotton past the blockade of Galveston and Sabine Pass. An order of August 9, 1864, from Lincoln to General E. R. S. Canby, in command of the military district, stipulated that Hamilton, or anyone authorized by him in writing, was to be allowed to control the shipment of cotton from the two ports.[27] Although Lincoln must have intended the permit as a favor, it is doubtful that Hamilton or anyone else profited from it.[28] The permit was revoked early in November, only three months after it was issued. Prompt and effective action would have been required for one shipload of cotton to have been moved. The permit was limited to Galveston and Sabine Pass, and neither was held by Union forces at the time. Moreover, it is doubtful that Union naval patrols would have honored the permit if they had intercepted a ship loaded with cotton.

In pledging himself to the Union cause and going north two years before, Hamilton had to leave his wife and children

25. New York *Tribune*, October 12, 14, 15, 17, 18, 19, 21, 22, 25, 26, 1864.
26. New Orleans *Picayune*, November 19, 29, 1864.
27. Roy Basler, *The Collected Works of Abraham Lincoln*, VII, pp. 488-489.
28. Howard K. Beale (ed.), *The Diary of Gideon Wells* (3 vols., W. W. Norton, New York, c. 1960), II, pp. 159, 162, 167; Howard K. Beale (ed.), "The Diary of Edward Bates," *Annual Report of the American Historical Association for the Year 1930*, IV, p. 414.

behind in Texas. His family continued to live on the farm east of the State Capitol; presumably they were able to survive from such mainstays as chickens and milk cows. Clothing was in short supply during the war and it is doubtful that the Hamilton family was able to buy much, if any. The late Mrs. John Chiles, Sr., granddaughter of the Hamiltons, remembered that the Hamilton boys, in addition to gardening, made shoes.[29] Besides providing for the needs of their family, it is possible that they produced a few extra pairs for sale to the public.

Hamilton was much concerned about the welfare of members of his family all during his exile from Texas.[30] He explored the possibility of bringing them out of Texas, apparently even before leaving Matamoros for New Orleans. There he requested the help of Governor Santiago Vidaurri of the Mexican States of Nuevo León and Coahuila. On November 10, 1862 Secretary of State Seward wrote to Governor Vidaurri about intervening with the Confederate Government in Texas on behalf of Hamilton's family. Consequently Governor Vidaurri on January 29, 1863, sent a letter to Brigadier General H. P. Bee, commander of the Confederate Military District of Texas, requesting his aid in getting Mrs. Hamilton and the children to New Orleans. Bee, on February 5, passed the request on to General Magruder, Confederate commander in Texas, who endorsed Bee's letter as follows: "The request will be granted solely out of respect to his Excellency Governor Vidaurri, unless his Excellency Governor Lubbock has some political reasons against it." Governor Vidaurri's original request of January 29, with the accompanying papers, was forwarded to Governor Lubbock.

In reply, Governor Lubbock remarked that although Hamilton had "deserted his country and allied himself to her enemies . . . [Lubbock] knew of no charges against Mrs. Hamilton sufficient to justify him in prohibiting her de-

29. Interview of John L. Waller, June 7, 1960, with Mrs. John Chiles, Sr., granddaughter of A. J. Hamilton.

30. President Lincoln, September 19, 1863, to General N. P. Banks, in Basler, *The Collected Works of Abraham Lincoln*, VI, p. 465.

parture." He added, however, that the request involved a military question, and that the decision was up to General Magruder. At the same time, Lubbock called attention to Hamilton's part in the threatened invasion of Texas, which might justify holding Mrs. Hamilton and the children as hostages to insure the good behavior of the invaders and the proper treatment of Texans.[31] Governor Lubbock delayed action almost six months.[32]

General Magruder announced on May 23, 1864, that he had acceded to the request, but there was a further delay of almost seven months.[33] In the meantime, during the summer of 1864, Mrs. Hamilton and the children suffered a serious setback in the loss of their home by fire. The cause is not known, and no charge of arson seems to have been filed. The loss was irreparable: the house and all of its contents—clothing, furniture, and utensils—seem to have been destroyed.[34]

At last, arrangements for the departure of the Hamilton family were consummated. Accompanied by Mrs. T. H. Duval and a Mrs. Stancel, Mrs. Hamilton and the children took passage on the U. S. transport *Clinton* bound for New Orleans. They arrived December 14, 1864, almost two years after Governor Vidaurri had interceded in their behalf. Since A. J. Hamilton was in New Orleans on November 29, it is virtually certain that he was there to meet his family.[35]

After two and one-half years of separation, this reunion must have been an ecstatic occasion. It appears likely that

31. War Department Collection of Confederate Records, R. G. 109, Union Provost Marshal Files, Box No. 154, A. G. O. Restriction, National Archives; J. L. Haynes to Governor A. J. Hamilton, June 13, 1863, in A. J. Hamilton Papers, Archives, University of Texas Library.

32. Mrs. Frank R. Lubbock to Provisional Governor A. J. Hamilton, September 25, 1865, in Governor Hamilton Correspondence (letters filed in envelope marked September 1-30, 1865; Executive Record Book, No. 281, p. 88—both in Archives Division, Texas State Library).

33. War Department Collection of Confederate Records, R. G. 109, Union Provost Marshal Files, Box No. 154, A. G. O. Restrictions, National Archives.

34. Interview with Mrs. John Chiles, Sr., June 7, 1960; also interview with Frank and Bessie Woodburn, April 29, 1962—all grandchildren of A. J. Hamilton; *State Gazette,* August 3, 1864.

35. New Orleans *Picayune,* December 14, 1864; *ibid.,* November 19, 29, 1864.

Hamilton spent not only Christmas, 1864, with his family, but the winter of 1864-1865 as well.

About the middle of May, 1865, Hamilton left New Orleans for another visit to Washington, D. C. Here on June 2, he had an interview with President Andrew Johnson, who had succeeded upon Lincoln's death, April 14. Fifteen days later, on June 17, the new President appointed Hamilton Provisional Governor of Texas. In commenting on this action, the New York *Tribune* referred to it as the "reappointment" of Hamilton, since President Lincoln had made known his wish that Hamilton serve in this position.[36] On June 19, 1865, Hamilton returned his commissions of Military Governor and Brigadier General to Secretary of War Stanton in order to assume his new duties as Provisional Governor.[37]

In Texas, military activities quickly ended after the surrender of General Lee on April 9, 1865. Nevertheless, Confederate General Edmund Kirby Smith, commander of the Trans-Mississippi Department, for several weeks acted under a delusion that he still led a well-armed, disciplined army of 50,000 men. However, after returning to his headquarters from an absence of only a few weeks, he found to his humiliation and dismay that these forces had practically disappeared. On June 2, 1865, he signed the terms that surrendered all forces under his command.[38]

Thus left without military authority—meaning almost no authority at all—Texas became the scene of pillaging, plundering, and even worse crimes. In some parts of the State, disorders reached alarming dimensions. These problems and others equally serious would immediately challenge the attention—and the statesmanship—of A. J. Hamilton, Provisional Governor. How effectively, and with what degree of restraint, would he exercise the immense power now resting in his hands?

36. New York *Tribune*, May 17, June 3, 19, 1865.
37. A. J. Hamilton, June 19, 1865, to President Andrew Johnson, per Secretary of War E. M. Stanton, in Records of the Adjutant General's Office, Commission Branch, 1865, H 497, Record Group 94, National Archives.
38. *O. R.*, Ser. I, Vol. XLVIII, Pt. I, pp. 191-194; *ibid.*, Pt. II, pp. 693, 727, 976.

CHAPTER V

Provisional Governor of Texas

THE COLLAPSE of the Confederacy was a severe shock to the people of Texas, and especially to their elected officials. A month before A. J. Hamilton was appointed Provisional Governor of Texas, Pendleton Murrah, Governor under the Confederacy, and his administrative assistants resolved, if at all possible, to avoid the humiliation of military occupation of their State. Governor Murrah dispatched W. P. Ballinger and Ashbel Smith to New Orleans as Commissioners of Texas to seek a conference with General E. R. S. Canby, Union commander of the Texas area. Ballinger and Smith were intelligent men of strong character; Governor Murrah hoped that they might persuade Canby to forego military occupation, by convincing him that the incumbent State Government of Texas was competent to continue functioning.

As a step in meeting the crisis that confronted the government, Governor Murrah issued two proclamations: one for assembling the Tenth Legislature in extraordinary session, with provision for an election to fill all vacancies in the Legislature itself; and the second for an election of delegates to a constitutional convention to assemble in Austin.[1]

As the commissioners from Texas sailed up the Mississippi River to New Orleans, they learned that General S. B. Buckner, agent of General E. Kirby Smith, Confederate commander of the Trans-Mississippi Department, had already agreed to terms of surrender for all Confederate forces in this area. Nevertheless, Ballinger and Smith requested a conference with General Canby who rather reluctantly consented. Before going

1. W. P. Ballinger, Diary, entries of May 17, 27, 29, 30; June 18, 1865; *War of Rebellion: Official Records of the Union and Confederate Armies* (130 vols., Washington, D.C., 1880-1901), Ser. I, Vol. XLVIII, Pt. II, p. 648. (Hereinafter cited as *O. R.*)

to the conference, held May 29, 1865, Ballinger had a long consultation with a leading Unionist, John Hancock, District Judge of the Second Judicial District in Texas. Judge Hancock told him that the Texas Unionists in New Orleans were divided over policy for Reconstruction in Texas. He asserted that a group of extremists, led by A. J. Hamilton, favored a harsh policy of vengeance and retribution. Since Hamilton had gone to Washington about the middle of May, Ballinger assumed that he was seeking appointment as Provisional Governor of Texas.[2]

On the basis of Judge Hancock's report, Ballinger distrusted and feared Hamilton. The commissioner expressed his sentiments in the conference with General Canby on May 29. In reply, the general suggested that Ballinger and Smith confer with General Phil Sheridan, who was now in command of all Union forces south and west of the Arkansas River. The meeting took place later, with Canby present. Both generals were courteous, but Sheridan made it clear that he intended to dispatch an occupation force to Texas. In fact, at an earlier date—May 9, 1865—Canby had assigned to General Gordon Granger the responsibility of organizing and commanding such a force. It appears that Smith and Ballinger were not informed of this decision. In keeping with his orders, Granger acted promptly; on June 17, at Galveston, he assumed command of all Federal forces in Texas.[3] Early in June, Sheridan ordered 8,000 cavalry troops to Texas, and before the end of the month an army of 32,000 men had been assigned to the force occupying the State.[4]

While these developments ensued, A. J. Hamilton was on his way to Texas, armed with a commission as Provisional Governor issued by Andrew Johnson, who had succeeded to the presidency on the death of Abraham Lincoln. Because of

2. Ballinger, Diary, entries shown in Reference 1 above; New York *Tribune*, May 17, 1865; *The Handbook of Texas* (2 vols., Austin, the Texas State Historical Association, 1952), I, 763.

3. Ballinger, Diary, entries, as shown above; *O. R.*, Ser. I., Vol. XLVIII, Pt. II, pp. 361, 476, 477.

4. *Ibid.*, pp. 476, 713, 865, 910, 922.

the difficulties of travel at the time, Hamilton was delayed in his journey; he reached Galveston on July 22, weeks after the Federal military was already firmly established in the State.[5]

While Texans were awaiting the arrival of the new Provisional Governor, there was much speculation about him and the policies he would follow. Epperson and Throckmorton, who had opposed secession but had served the Confederacy, were quite apprehensive of Hamilton's attitude; they therefore concerned themselves with finding means to control the newly appointed State executive.[6] As for the press, Editor Robert W. Loughery of the *Texas Republican* wrote an editorial to the effect that Hamilton now had an opportunity to render a real service to the suffering and distressed people of Texas, who had honored him in the past.[7] Editor Willard Richardson of the Galveston *News* published the comments of a contributor who claimed to have had an interview recently with Hamilton. The writer said that the new Governor gave every assurance of having only affection for the people of Texas, and of having no desire to hurt or humiliate them in any way.[8] A private citizen, a rich merchant and landowner of Austin who knew Hamilton, expressed a similarly favorable opinion. This man, S. M. Swenson, was convinced that the Provisional Governor would not be vengeful. Although aware of Hamilton's "occasional irregular habits"—overindulgence in beer and whiskey—Swenson admired and trusted Hamilton. On June 17, 1865, Swenson wrote to E. M. Pease, expressing full confidence in Hamilton and urging Pease to support him.[9] This Pease was to do loyally and ef-

5. New York *Tribune,* June 3, 19, 1865; *Flake's Bulletin* (Galveston, Texas), July 22, 24, 28, 1865; *O. R.,* Ser. I, Vol. XLVIII, Pt. II, pp. 361, 476, 713, 910, 922.

6. B. H. Epperson to J. W. Throckmorton, June 18, 24, 1865, in J. W. Throckmorton Correspondence, Archives, University of Texas.

7. *Texas Republican* (Marshall, Texas), June 30, 1865.

8. Galveston *News,* May 5, June 9, July 10 1865.

9. S. M. Swenson to E. M. Pease, June 17, 1865, in Graham-Pease Collection, Archives, Austin Public Library.

fectively after Hamilton had assumed control of the Governor's office in Austin.

Moving from Galveston to Houston, Hamilton was greeted by the leading citizens, who honored him with a banquet. Unfortunately, his address on this occasion gave to many of his listeners little cause for satisfaction. They had hoped that he would announce his support of a plan for gradual emancipation. Instead, Hamilton made it all too clear that as far as he was concerned, slavery had ended. In addition, he made some remarks which P. W. Gray, a member of the House of Representatives of the First Congress of the Confederate States of America, described in a letter to former Governor E. M. Pease as "unnecessarily harsh, bitter and denunciatory," remarks that "irritated many favorably disposed to meet him more than half-way—injured his own interests and cannot, so far as I can see, do good." In discussing the question of social equality, Hamilton declared sharply, "I am willing to take my chances with the Blacks." Gray saw danger in Hamilton's attitude and expressed the hope that Pease would be able to induce Hamilton to tone down his speeches.[10]

Pease and another of Hamilton's old friends, George W. Paschal, were in charge of a rousing welcome in Austin for the Provisional Governor, on August 2. An immense crowd greeted Hamilton, not as a stranger newly arrived but as a fellow Texan, long absent from his own home. A huge, colorful parade—in which appeared the military escort of Governor Hamilton, sent from Galveston on orders of General Sheridan, area commander—emphasized the importance of the occasion.

The address of welcome was delivered by E. M. Pease, who tried to strike a note of conciliation and goodwill. He declared that the people of Texas:

Without regard to their past opinions upon those questions that have involved our country in all the horrors of civil war during the last four years, they now acquiesce in the result of that war, and cheerfully accept the consequences that legitimately flow from it, with a full ap-

10. P. W. Gray to E. M. Pease, July 28, 1865, in *ibid.*

preciation of the sacrifices of feeling and of old habits that many of them are required to make. They are prepared to resume their allegiance to the United States, satisfied that in doing so nothing is demanded from them that is calculated to destroy their self-respect or to humiliate them in the opinions of the world. While they receive and welcome you as the Representative of the United States, invested with the authority to re-establish civil government over them, they recognize in you a fellow-citizen who has long been identified with them in sympathy and interest, one whom they have heretofore favored with high public station, and to whom they now look with confidence to pursue such a course of policy as will secure a restoration of law and order and a prompt and impartial administration of justice.

Pease's words constituted a generous statement from a broadminded, kindly man. Governor Hamilton, however, did not react in the manner that his listeners expected. It is true that he thanked Pease and stated that he came as a friend. But, changing his tone, he bitterly assailed those who had brought Texas to its present state of affairs. He reminded his audience of his warnings in 1860-61; he recalled the part his hearers had played in trying to rend the greatest nation on earth—one that had never exacted a cent of direct taxes from them or oppressed them in any manner. Furthermore, he reminded them of his warning that they would surely suffer from military oppression and crushing taxation if they failed to heed his advice. Although eloquent and forceful, Hamilton sounded vengeful. To many listeners, his remarks did not augur well for the people of Texas. Editor Loughery of the *Texas Republican* considered the speech a harangue. Yet other editors endorsed Hamilton's position: for example, Frank Brown of the *Southern Intelligencer* and N. C. Raymond, who edited the *State Gazette* for a few months in 1865. *Flake's Bulletin* also supported Hamilton.[11]

Hamilton had made good use of the three days he had spent in Galveston the preceding month. In addition to holding regular office hours, during which he was deluged with

11. *Southern Intelligencer* (Austin), August 4, 1865; *O. R.*, Ser. I, Vol. XLVIII, Pt. II, p. 1069; *State Gazette,* August 1, 8, 15, 1865; *Texas Republican,* August 8, 1865.

visitors, he had issued on July 24 a "Proclamation to the People of Texas." In it he had announced his appointment as Provisional Governor and outlined his objectives. According to his view, all acts of the State Legislature passed during the war must be repudiated as null and void; the wartime constitution of the State must be supplanted by a new one drafted by delegates loyal to the Union, chosen by the loyal citizens of Texas.

The proclamation also declared that slavery no longer existed. The slave owners had waged war against the government that had previously sustained slavery; the contest was one of mortal combat and it had resulted in the destruction of the institution of slavery forever. Moreover, unless the new constitution of the State clearly forbade slavery, and unless the Legislature enacted proper laws concerning the freedmen, representatives and senators from Texas would never be seated in Congress. Hamilton's proclamation received warm support from *Flake's Bulletin*, the *Southern Intelligencer*, and, for a short time, the *State Gazette*. But the reaction from the Galveston *News*, the Houston *Telegraph*, and the *Texas Republican* was the opposite.[12]

Regardless of his opinions and views of those differing with him, Hamilton was obliged immediately to cope with urgent practical problems. The first of these was to establish civil government at all levels. After the Confederate Governor, Murrah, had become convinced that he could do no more to influence events, he had abandoned his office and left Austin. There was great confusion in the Capital, and similar conditions prevailed in other parts of Texas. In some of the counties, officials had given up their posts and these had to be filled.[13] In addition, there was a near-breakdown of all means for disseminating information, including the suspension of

12. Executive Record Book, No. 281, pp. 26, 192-194, Archives Division, Texas State Library; *Flake's Bulletin*, July 27, 28, 31, 1865; *Southern Intelligencer*, August 2, 1865; *State Gazette*, August 1, 1865.

13. Election Register, No. 260, 1860-1865, arranged by counties throughout the volume, Archives Division Texas State Library.

many of the local weekly newspapers. The mail service was practically inoperative.[14]

Yet, the news of Hamilton's arrival in Austin, and of the great power that he would exercise, soon became known throughout the State. Many citizens, alerted by the news, came to see him personally, and many others wrote to him. Among the most important persons to call on the new Governor was J. W. Throckmorton, previously mentioned as a leading Unionist, who had chosen to serve the Confederate Government after the voters had approved the Ordinance of Secession. He was to play a prominent, though not always constructive, role in Reconstruction. Occasionally, Throckmorton would be afflicted with spells of disillusionment resulting from the acts of the "hell-hounds of Radicalism." At such times, he would threaten to retire into the bosom of his family, but these expressions were sheer pretense, for he was ablaze with political ambition.[15]

Throckmorton came to Austin to carry out, if possible, the plan to control Hamilton that he and Ben H. Epperson had conceived in their June correspondence. As their strategy unfolded its main points were to induce Hamilton to retain all county and local officials and to assemble a constitutional convention at an early date, possibly in October.[16] The proposal to retain all officials was altogether unrealistic. In some cases the officers had abandoned their posts. Furthermore, in certain areas such as Throckmorton's own section of North Texas, divisions in sentiment as to secession had been deep, and severe persecution of Unionists had ensued. In other parts of the State, especially in the predominantly German communities, differences had likewise arisen, and much bitterness still remained.[17]

14. W. M. Daily, Special Agent U.S. Post Office Department, to Provisional Governor A. J. Hamilton, in Governors' Letters (Hamilton), Texas State Library.
15. J. W. Throckmorton to B. H. Epperson, January 21, 1866, in Ben H. Epperson Papers, Archives, University Texas Library.
16. B. H. Epperson to J. W. Throckmorton, June 18, 24, 1865, in J. W. Throckmorton Correspondence, Archives, University of Texas Library.
17. Frank Smyrl, "Abolitionism, Unionism, and Vigilantism" (M. A. thesis, University of Texas, 1961), Ch. VI.

When Hamilton for seemingly good reasons turned down the proposals of Throckmorton, the latter flew into an intemperate rage. During this fit of anger, he wrote his friend Epperson that Hamilton was determined to remove all incumbent officials, carrying out a policy of vengeance.[18]

Throckmorton's accusation was ill-founded. Hamilton did not dismiss officials in a wholesale manner; on the contrary, he retained many of the elected officials, often over vigorous protests. Besides, he frequently appointed persons that Throckmorton and Epperson recommended. Hamilton did name a completely new set of district judges and district attorneys; but a number of these, including Richard Coke, an enthusiastic secessionist, had served the Confederate Government.[19]

Hamilton's efforts at fairness in making appointments is illustrated by his decision concerning James Wiley Magoffin of El Paso County. A strong supporter of the Confederacy, Magoffin had been deeply involved in providing supplies for Colonel John R. Baylor, who had led the Texas Mounted Rifles in their efforts to occupy New Mexico. Magoffin, a clever and friendly man, won the friendship of A. J. Hamilton and his family. The Governor concluded that the estimable old gentleman, if a participant in the war, must have been a victim of circumstances—not a rebel at heart. Hamilton therefore not only gave Magoffin a commission to raise a small military force to aid the local officials in law enforcement, but also authorized him to name the new officials for El Paso County.[20]

Appointments of this kind displeased the Unionists in El Paso and elsewhere in Texas; in fact, many Unionists protested bitterly against them. In some instances, the protests

18. Throckmorton to Epperson, August 8, 27, 1865, and January 21, 1866, in B. H. Epperson Papers, Archives University of Texas Library.

19. Letters from Epperson and Throckmorton to Governor Hamilton during fall of 1865, in Governors' Letters (Hamilton); Election Register, No. 260, 1860-1865, p. 41, and throughout the volume—both in Archives Division, Texas State Library.

20. J. W. Magoffin to Governor Hamilton, December 6, 1865, and a strong protest from a group in El Paso, in Governors' Letters (Hamilton); Governor Hamilton to J. W. Magoffin, November 15, 1865, in Executive Record Book, No. 281, p. 119—both in Archives Division, Texas State Library.

were effective. For example, when it was brought to Hamilton's attention that William H. Hord, chief justice of Dallas County, was an unreconstructed secessionist, he speedily revoked Hord's commission.[21]

In making appointments, Hamilton was occasionally motivated by personal considerations. Not adverse to appointing his own brothers, he named Hezekiah B. Hamilton wreckmaster of Cameron County[22] and sent Morgan C. Hamilton to England on a special mission. The mission was to recover the indemnity bonds that the Texas State Military Board had transferred during the war to that country.[23] James M. Swisher had carried the indemnity bonds to England for the Texas Military Board. A. J. Hamilton now appointed him agent for Texas to dispose of the Salt Works, the Jordan Salines of Van Zandt County.[24]

A friend of Throckmorton and Epperson, James H. Bell, became Secretary of State.[25] Albert H. Latimer, sponsored by Epperson, was named Comptroller.[26] Hamilton retained his affection for his friends and former colleagues John H. Reagan and A. W. Terrell. When William Reagan, brother of John H., came to Austin with a list of names proposed for appointment as officials of Falls County, Hamilton made him chief justice of that county. J. C. Terrell, brother of A. W., submitted to Hamilton a list of names for the offices in Tarrant County; it won immediate and complete approval.[27]

The State Government that Hamilton undertook to direct had fallen into near chaos. Typical of the conditions that prevailed: the roof of the Capitol was leaking badly and the entire building was in bad repair. The treasury of the State

21. Election Register, No. 260, 1860-1865, pp. 241-243-245, Archives Division, Texas State Library.
22. *Ibid.*, p. 4.
23. Executive Record Book No 281, pp. 75-76 Archives, Texas State Library.
24. *Ibid.*, pp. 35-36.
25. Election Register, No. 260, 1860-1865, p. 33, Archives, Texas State Library.
26. *Ibid.*
27. *Ibid.*, pp. 281, 283, 727, 731.

had been robbed of several thousand dollars. On learning of this loss, Hamilton appointed two trusted friends, E. M. Pease and Swante Palm, to investigate the fiscal situation. Their findings were dismal, if not shocking.[28]

An undated preliminary report by Pease and Palm is in the correspondence file of Governor Hamilton for August 1-15, 1865. It shows that the State Treasury had total assets of approximately $6,900 in specie; $800 in Louisiana bank bills; and 106 U. S. indemnity bonds, each with a face value of $1,000; plus $23,975 interest, accumulated at 5 per cent on the bonds.[29]

In their final report, Pease and Palm revealed that the Texas Military Board had withdrawn more than five hundred indemnity bonds that had belonged to the School Fund, and dissipated them. Three hundred of the bonds, and a large number of coupons representing collectible interest, were in the possession of two houses in Manchester, England, Droege and Company and Peabody and Company. Twenty of the bonds were held by Oliver and Brothers, Monterrey, Mexico. Others had been sold, and still others turned over to different parties.

Nineteen of the indemnity bonds had simply disappeared: a former member of the defunct Texas Military Board claimed that he had sent them to M. T. Johnson, prominent business-man and politician of Tarrant County and a member of the Texas Secession Convention; but Johnson denied ever having received them. As late as December 24, 1875, Governor Richard Coke pointed out to the Texas delegation in Congress that twenty-one of the missing bonds had never been pre-sented to the United States Treasury for payment; he asked what could be done about recovering their value. It appeared that nineteen of the twenty-one bonds were those that al-legedly had been sent to M. T. Johnson.[30]

28. Executive Record Book No. 281, pp. 37-38, Archives, Texas State Library.
29. Governors' Letters (Hamilton, August 1-15, 1865), Archives Division, Texas State Library.
30. Executive Record Book No. 281, pp. 94-119, Archives, Texas State Library.

ANDREW JACKSON HAMILTON
Military Governor of Texas, Brigadier General

Governor's Mansion, Austin, Texas, 1866

PRESIDENT ABRAHAM LINCOLN

*Appointed Hamilton a Military
Governor of Texas and
Brigadier General of
Volunteers.*

SALMON P. CHASE

*Secretary of the Treasury
under Lincoln. As Chief Justice
of the United States,
appointed Hamilton
Register of Bankruptcy
in 1867.*

EDMUND J. DAVIS

*Last of the Reconstruction
Governors of Texas*

MORGAN C. HAMILTON

*Republican United States
Senator from Texas,
1870-1877*

MARY JANE (BOWEN) HAMILTON
*Mrs. A. J. Hamilton in her
early sixties*

Mrs. Hamilton and one of her pet Jersey cows

"FAIR OAKS"

Home built by A. J. Hamilton in the early 1870s
(Painting by Griffith Gates)

Hamilton's Pool — Refuge of A. J. Hamilton on flight north

ELISHA MARSHALL PEASE

Provisional Governor,
1867-1869
Appointed by General
Phil Sheridan

ALEXANDER WATKINS TERRELL

Law Partner of Hamilton
in the 1850s

ORAN MILO ROBERTS

President of Secession
Convention of 1861

SVANTE MAGNUS SWENSON
Merchant and large landowner

JAMES WEBB THROCKMORTON
Thirteenth Governor, 1866-67

Removed from office by General Phil Sheridan

GEORGE W. PASCHAL
Lawyer and Editor

The A. J. Hamilton Funeral Cortege at Texas State Capitol

The disappearance of another lot of indemnity bonds was especially significant, since the legal questions involved led to a famous decision of the United States Supreme Court. On March 12, 1865—only four weeks before Lee surrendered —the Texas Military Board turned over 135 bonds to George W. White and John Chiles on their promise to provide the State with cotton cards and medicines in exchange. The bonds, including coupons, were worth more than $156,000. The two contractors agreed that in the event they failed to fulfill their obligation, they would repay the State in its own bonds and warrants, to be accepted at 100 cents on the dollar, in exchange for the indemnity bonds and coupons, to be valued at 80 cents on the dollar.[31] Considering the rapidly deteriorating fortunes of the Confederacy and the practical worthlessness of the State warrants at the time, this agreement of the board was indeed strange. Governor J. W. Throckmorton, Hamilton's successor, was right in saying, "The terms of the contract . . . indicate anything but a just contract."[32]

Despite these favorable terms, White wanted an even better deal. He requested and was awarded as an outright gift seventy-six of the indemnity bonds which were held by Droege and Company, in Manchester, England; but neither White nor Chiles received any of these bonds. White suggested that the contract be burned; for this reason, only outlines of its terms have been found.[33] On August 30, 1865, Governor Hamilton wrote President Johnson an account of the transaction with White and Chiles. Pointing out that they had fulfilled no part of their contract with the State, he requested the President to direct the Army to arrest the two men and send them back to Texas.[34]

On August 30, Governor Hamilton appointed George W. Paschal as agent for the state, dispatching him to Washington

31. *Ibid.* Texas v. White *Texas Reports,* XXV, p. 434; 7 Wall, 700-743.

32. Governor Throckmorton to Eleventh Legislature, Executive Record Book, No. 84, 39-55, Archives Division, Texas State Library.

33. Texas v. White, *Texas Reports,* XXV, p. 434, 7 Wall, 700.

34. Executive Record Book No. 281, pp. 38-44, Archives, Texas State Library.

to aid in recovering the bonds.[35] Hamilton also wrote Secretary of the Treasury Hugh McCulloch an account of the disposition of the various lots of the bonds and urged him not to make any payments on them—either principal or interest—except to the State of Texas.[36]

On September 26, 1865, Paschal wrote a detailed letter to R. W. Taylor, Comptroller of the United States, in which he gave a connected history of the problem. The letter indicated that the Secretary of the Treasury had been given notice during the war of the manner in which the Texas Military Board was using the indemnity bonds. Paschal added that in a conversation with him, White had said that he had bought $12,000 worth of fine brandies, and had offered the liquor to Governor Pendleton Murrah. After the Governor had declined it, White had used it himself.[37] When Governor Hamilton heard the rumor of the brandy purchases, he issued to the sheriff of Travis County a warrant for the search of White's premises in Austin. After the sheriff completed the search, he reported finding six dozen bottles of the liquor.[38]

The State of Texas on February 15, 1867, six months after Hamilton had left the Governor's office, filed suit against White, Chiles and others for recovery of the bonds and coupons in question. The important case of *Texas v. George W. White, John P. Chiles, et al.,* was finally decided by the United States Supreme Court on April 15, 1869. George W. Paschal, as agent for the State and with the aid of three Washington attorneys, won a clear-cut victory on the legal principles involved. The victory was notable as far as the fees of the attorneys and their legal reputations were concerned; but for

35. *Ibid.,* p. 38.   36. *Ibid.,* p. 45.

37. George W. Paschal to R. W. Taylor, Comptroller of the United States, September 26, 28, 1865, in Governors' Letters (Hamilton), Archives Division, Texas State Library.

38. Governor Hamilton to Sheriff Thomas C. Collins, September 1, 1865, Executive Record Book No. 281, p. 46, Archives Division, Texas State Library; Sheriff Collins' report of the same date in Governors' Letters (Hamilton), Archives Division, Texas State Library.

39. 7 Wall, 700-734; 10 Wall (*In Re Paschal*), 483-497.

the Government of Texas, the decision left much to be desired. The State recovered only fifty of the bonds that were brought under the jurisdiction of the Court.[39]

Although the legal action in *Texas v. White* did not benefit the State financially as Hamilton had expected, the decision of the Supreme Court was of basic importance in other respects. In effect, the court used the case to affirm the constitutional theory of Lincoln regarding the nature of the Union. Lincoln's thesis, which Hamilton consistently supported, held that the Union was indissoluble and that Texas and the other Southern States had never legally seceded from it. In handing down the decision, Chief Justice Salmon P. Chase referred to the Articles of Confederation, which, according to its provisions, created a "perpetual Union," and to the Constitution, ordained "to form a more perfect Union." He concluded: "The Constitution, in all of its provisions, looks to an indestructible union, composed of indestructible states." Since Texas, in spite of the Act of Secession, had remained in the Union as a State, its government was legally competent to appear as a party before the Court in a suit to recover the bonds in question.[40]

While occupied with the problem of recovering the indemnity bonds, Governor Hamilton sought to locate and recoup other properties of the State which had been lost or misappropriated during the war and immediately thereafter. Many of these assets, especially cotton, had been scattered by pillaging soldiers and civilians during the period of confusion resulting from the military collapse. Although Hamilton's efforts were complicated by the presence of United States Treasury agents over the State, he was able to effect some recoveries.[41] For example, he arranged for Texas to receive a credit of $24,000 for cotton sent to Swenson, Perkins and Company of New Orleans. He sought also to liquidate an assignment of some $60,000 from J. L. Williams to Pendleton Murrah, last Gover-

40. 7 Wall, 700-734.
41. *Southern Intelligencer,* November 23, 1865; Adjutant General's Office, Department of Texas (Old Books, 4, 9, 21), National Archives.

nor of Texas during the war, but it is doubtful if the State ever benefited from it.[42]

With the Treasury of the State almost empty, Hamilton was faced with the urgent problem of raising money to restore the operations of the government. Since the credit of Texas was nil, the only means open to him was taxation. Faced with this emergency, he might have exercised the taxing power drastically; instead, he acted with notable restraint. He fixed the tax rate for State purposes at only 12½ mills on each $100 valuation of property. This small tax was promptly collected, and it provided funds sufficient for current needs.[43]

While financial problems of the kind described pressed for solution, the Provisional Governor was obliged to direct his attention to other serious matters. Among these was the breakdown of authority and the increase of crime throughout much of Texas. Even before the war, lawlessness was all too prevalent; it had increased greatly during the period of hostilities and even more following Lee's surrender. Hamilton's files contain many letters and reports on this subject from almost every section of the State. The district judges, in particular, were acquainted with and disturbed by the conditions that prevailed, and a number of them wrote reports to the Governor. A few examples may be mentioned.

Judge William W. Wallace of the Fifth Judicial District, in deep East Texas, on December 18, 1865, reported much crime in the Big Thicket area of Sabine and Angelina counties. On November 30, December 7, 1865, and again on February 2, 1866, Judge B. W. Gray of the Eighth Judicial District complained bitterly to Hamilton of his troubles with United States Treasury Agents and military officials. Additional reports came to the Governor regarding crime and violence along the Red River border; Caldwell County was often in a state of turbulence.[44] Some writers expressed uneasiness over

42. Statement of S. M. Swenson, N. O., December 20, 1865; John L. Williams, Assignment, copy in Governors' Letters (Hamilton)—both in Archives Division.
43. Executive Record Book No. 281, p. 50, Archives Division, Texas State Library.
44. Governor Hamilton to General Phil Sheridan, January 7, 1866; Judge W. W.

the Governor's generous attitude regarding amnesty; they voiced the fear that the Secessionists would soon regain power and begin persecution of both the freedmen and the Unionists.[45]

A serious threat to the security of many communities was clearly apparent: the breakdown of the courts and the administration of the law. The court dockets over the State were crowded with cases that had been "sleeping" for some time because of the confusion that the war had entailed. Governor Hamilton attacked this problem directly—he urged the judges to move with dispatch in the trial of cases.[46] He also, somewhat hesitantly, authorized the enlistment of local groups to aid elected officials in law enforcement; at the same time, he was careful to specify that any persons so deputized must be subject to the control of elected officials.[47]

At first, Hamilton was inclined to exclude from court practice all lawyers who required presidential amnesty and had not yet received it. After hearing the opinion of E. M. Pease, however, Hamilton agreed to permit attorneys who had taken the oath of allegiance to practice, subject to the discretion of the district judges.[48] The need for attorneys to assist in the urgent work of bringing court dockets up to date was too great to be impeded by a political technicality. Hamilton assisted the courts in another way. In order to give their authority his firm backing, he exercised the pardoning power with great care. In fact, he issued pardons only in exceptional cases—only when he was convinced that a conviction rested

Wallace to Governor Hamilton, December 18, 1865; Judge B. W. Gray to Governor Hamilton, November 30, December 7, 1865, February 2, 1866—all in Governors' Letters (Hamilton), Archives Division, Texas State Library.

45. D. J. Baldwin to Governor Hamilton, November 7, 1865, in *ibid.*

46. Governor Hamilton's Proclamations of September 8, *re* collection of debts; September 25, 1865, *re* court procedures and collection of debts, in Executive Record Book No. 281, pp. 52, 71-74, Archives Division, Texas State Library.

47. *Ibid.*, pp. 132-133.

48. Proclamation of September 18, 1865, concerning judicial affairs, Executive Record Book No. 281, pp. 52-54, 137-138, Archives Division, Texas State Library; E. M. Pease to Governor Hamilton, November 8, 1865, in Governors' Letters (Hamilton)—all in Archives Division, Texas State Library.

on inadequate or confusing evidence, or that excessive punishment had been imposed.[49]

Indian raids constituted still another worry for the Governor. During this unsettled period, the Indians along the frontier took full advantage of the weakened defenses of the white settlements. Hamilton received many appeals for help. Thus, Judge R. W. Scott of the Sixteenth Judicial District and other citizens in the area urged relief for Parker County and the counties adjoining it.[50] The Governor replied that he had been pressing this problem upon the military for weeks. Explaining that the State Treasury was depleted, he called attention to the act passed by the Legislature, February 7, 1861, authorizing frontier counties to form companies of Minute Men as a means of defense against Indian raids.[51]

Recognizing the seriousness of the menace, Hamilton wrote to General Phil Sheridan to insure continued occupation of Texas by Federal forces. In his letter, Hamilton insisted that in view of the crime, violence, and frontier disturbances then prevailing, Union soldiers should not be removed from the State. Sheridan responded favorably but added that the matter would have to be referred to General U. S. Grant. Hamilton also wrote for help to General H. G. Wright, who had relieved General Gordon Granger as commander of the Federal forces in Texas. Wright was willing to use what troops he had, but stated that Sheridan would have to approve any action.[52] To leave no stone unturned, Hamilton appealed to General George A. Custer, in charge of the cavalry, requesting him to make a demonstration along the threatened frontiers of Parker, Wise, and Jack counties. This Custer agreed to do.[53] Efforts of this

49. Executive Record Book No. 281, pp. 151, 157, 158, 170, 178, 187, 188, Archives Division, Texas State Library.

50. Judge R. W. Scott to Governor Hamilton, October 3, 1865, Governors' Letters (Hamilton), Archives Division, Texas State Library.

51. *Ibid.;* H. P. N. Gammel (comp.), *Laws of Texas* (10 vols., Austin, 1898), V, p. 346.

52. Governor Hamilton to General Phil Sheridan, January 7, 1866; General H. G. Wright to Governor Hamilton, August 14, September 2, 1865—both in Governors' Letters (Hamilton), Archives Division, Texas State Library.

53. Custer to Governor Hamilton, November 23, 1865, January 12, 1866, in *ibid.*

kind were doubtless of some value, but the Indian problem would remain unsolved for many years.

While facing up to the challenges mentioned, Hamilton received numerous letters that reflected the interests, attitudes, and problems of the people of Texas as they emerged from the war into the uncertain era of Reconstruction. Some old friends of his wrote about their troubles; still others wrote in behalf of a son, a relative, or a neighbor; others wrote only to wish him well. George W. Brackenridge, who later became a noted regent and benefactor of The University of Texas, wanted to name the officials for Jackson County on the Gulf Coast. Several women sent messages. One of these correspondents was Mrs. M. L. Poland, a friend of the Hamilton family. After hearing his speches in Galveston and Austin, she requested him to refrain from making further remarks until he could eliminate the bitterness they expressed. She added, significantly, that she was "a Southern woman who now had to prepare her own breakfast."

Still another woman, Lucy M. Latimer, wrote the Governor a strong plea for the control of grog shops, which she asserted "made more widows than war, pestilence, or famine." In view of Hamilton's "occasional irregular habits," one wonders how he reacted to this appeal. A letter of a different kind came from Mrs. Francis R. Lubbock, wife of the former confederate Governor of Texas. She requested permission from Governor Hamilton to go north in order to join her husband, who was a prisoner in Fort Delaware. Her request was granted immediately; in addition, Hamilton called on all officials to aid Mrs. Lubbock in every way possible. This action stood in sharp contrast to that of Governor Lubbock himself on a somewhat similar request made in behalf of Mrs. A. J. Hamilton during the war.[54]

In addition to these personal, individual concerns, unresolved political questions loomed ahead at all times during these trying days. How could civil government be reestablished? How could Texas be restored to the Union? Hamilton

54. *Ibid.* August-September, 1865.

gave continuous attention to these and similar problems. After he had been in Austin only a month, he issued in September, 1865, another "Proclamation to the People of Texas," in which he reiterated most of the points covered in his earlier proclamations and speeches. He emphasized the point that he wanted his objectives understood as they related to the restoration of civil government to the people of Texas, and to the restoration of the State to the National Federation. He insisted that the people of Texas should realize that slavery was ended and that the Negroes must be protected in their freedom. Moreover, he declared that it was necessary for the loyal citizens of the State to control the election of delegates to a convention which must be held to deal with basic constitutional questions.[55]

While Hamilton was convinced that Texas faced fundamental political and social changes, he was determined that they should occur in as orderly a manner as possible. When rumors began to circulate to the effect that the Negroes were to receive free land and livestock, he decided to destroy this strange delusion. He accordingly delivered, on November 17, 1865, "An Address to the Freedmen of Texas" on the subject. He was so anxious that they clearly understand his position that he sent copies of the statement to the chief justices of the various counties, requesting them to assemble the Negroes of their districts and read the address to them, with full explanations.

In essence, the proclamation contained expressions of friendship and admiration for the manner in which the freedmen had conducted themselves, plus hopes for their future prosperity and happiness. But at the same time, the Governor wanted the Negroes to understand that no land or "other things" would be given to them. He said specifically: "The United States Government has no land in Texas to give you . . . none will be taken from the white people to give to you." The freedmen, he went on, must work, make themselves valuable

55. Executive Record Book No. 281, pp. 55-71, Archives Division, Texas State Library.

to their employers, and save their earnings if they were to acquire lands and other property. Idleness and wandering about over the country would surely get them into trouble with the State Government.

This clear and unequivocal statement shows that Hamilton's position on the question of race relations was a conservative one. The assertions that he favored instant equality, the breaking down of all social barriers, were patently false.[56] His attitude on these and related issues will become clearer as attention is turned to Hamilton's role in writing a new constitution for Texas—a subject to be taken up in the following chapter.

56. Proclamation to Freedmen, November 17, 1865, in *ibid.,* pp. 129-131, Archives Division, Texas State Library.

CHAPTER VI

Hamilton's Reconstruction Program

IN THE OPENING PARAGRAPH of Hamilton's Proclamation to the People of Texas, issued in Galveston, July 25, 1865, he had announced his position on Reconstruction. The Provisional Governor had stated that his instructions from President Andrew Johnson at the time of his appointment were specific: they directed him to bring about the restoration of the former constitutional relations of Texas with the United States.[1] In pursuance of these instructions, Hamilton promptly attempted to follow the procedure which President Lincoln had recommended in his Amnesty Proclamation of December 10, 1863; President Johnson had supplemented the procedure after he succeeded Lincoln.

By the provisions of the Amnesty Proclamation, when citizens in any State in a number equal to as much as ten per cent of the voting population in 1860 had taken an oath of loyalty to the United States, elections would be held. These restored voters might proceed to reorganize their State; the President would then recognize the reorganized government of that State. Of course, as President Johnson pointed out, he could not guarantee the admission to Congress of those representatives of the newly franchised voters thus elected to that body, for Congress itself was the sole judge of the qualifications of its members. The plan of the supplemented Amnesty Proclamation of 1863 would restore the voting rights of most Confederate adult males—all but the Confederate political leaders, those who had relinquished high offices in the Federal Government, military officers in the Southern armed forces above the rank of colonel, and a few other speci-

1. Provisional Governor Hamilton's "Proclamation of July 25, 1865, to the People of Texas," in Executive Record Book, No. 281, pp. 26, 192-194, Archives Divison, Texas State Library.

fied groups. These must first apply to the President for individual pardon; only after receiving such pardon would former high-ranking Confederates be granted amnesty and regain the franchise.[2]

After some fulminations about "making treason odious," President Johnson had adopted the moderate policy of Lincoln; but he added several other classes of persons excepted from general amnesty, the most notable being holders of property with a value of $20,000 or more.[3] Governor Hamilton was expected to act on—that is, approve or disapprove—all applications for presidential amnesty in Texas. That there were possibilities of abuse, even corruption, in the administration of this system of amnesty cannot be doubted. The belief spread throughout the South that thousands of citizens suffered outrageous extortions in obtaining amnesty. Hamilton did not escape suspicion and covert charges of extortion; many Southerners felt that pardon brokers, with whom the Governor directly or indirectly associated, reaped fortunes in this field.[4]

In reviewing the records of this period, the present author has found no suggestion, much less evidence, that Governor Hamilton profited in any way from processing applications for amnesty. A careful study of the Amnesty Records for Texas in the National Archives, as well as sources in Texas, discloses that there were three well-known pardon brokers who operated successfully in the State: William Pitt Ballinger, George W. Paschal, and James Masterson.[5] These men were able to secure amnesty for various clients.

W. P. Ballinger, leading Galveston lawyer, a Unionist at

2. Samuel Eliot Morison and Henry Steele Commager, *The Growth of the American Republic* (2 vols., New York, Oxford Press, 1950), II, p. 32.

3. *Ibid.,* II, pp. 34-37.

4. J. T. Dorris, "Pardon Seekers and Brokers: A Sequel to Appomattox." *Journal of Southern History,* L, pp. 276-292; *Austin Republican,* June, 1869.

5. W. P. Ballinger, Diary, entries from August 5 through November 10, 1865, Archives, University of Texas Library; Amnesty Papers, Texas, Office of the Adjutant General, R G 94, Box Nos. 51-54, National Archives; R. Niles Graham-Elisha Marshall Pease Collection, Archives, Austin Public Library.

heart, served the Confederacy as Receiver and as legal adviser. After giving some thought to the idea of leaving the State, he decided to remain and apply for amnesty. If granted amnesty, he intended to return to his legal practice.[6] He had known Hamilton as a colleague of the bar before the war. Though feeling that the Governor was somewhat unstable in his principles, Ballinger considered him not "a bad or vindictive man."[7] Upon Hamilton's arrival as Provisional Governor in Galveston on July 22, 1865, Ballinger had readied his application for amnesty. In an interview with the Governor, Ballinger was successful in obtaining approval of his application, as well as the applications of a number of his clients. Thereafter, Ballinger went to Washington, D. C., to present these applications to the President. In this endeavor, Ballinger enlisted the assistance of his influential brother-in-law, Samuel R. Miller, Associate Justice of the United States Supreme Court, and of his uncle, Green Adams, former Congressman.[8]

A letter from Justice Miller to Secretary of State William H. Seward won Ballinger an interview which was cordial to the point that Seward wrote a note to President Johnson in Ballinger's behalf. As a result, the visiting Texan promptly conferred with the President, who informed him that his amnesty, on the suggestion of Seward, had already been granted.[9] Ballinger now had an entree almost at will to President Johnson and could present the applications of his clients with minimal delay. Not long after he began his amnesty work, Ballinger met George W. Paschal, prominent lawyer and editor from Austin; thereafter, the two Texans collaborated in handling a number of applications.[10] The fee that the pardon brokers charged each applicant was apparent-

6. Ballinger, Diary, special comments at end of 1860, and entries of May 17, 29, 30, August 7, 19, 21, 31, October 3, 24, 28-31, 1861; February 12, March 12, 1862; September 27, October 4, 21, November 13, 22, 1863; February 22, 1864; June 15, 1865.
7. W. P. Ballinger to Guy M. Bryan, June 17, 1865, in Guy M. Bryan Papers, Archives, University of Texas Library.
8. Ballinger, Diary, entries of August 8, 25, 1865.
9. *Ibid.*, August 22-28, 1865.
10. *Ibid.*, entry of September 30, 1865.

ly based on his ability to pay. Ballinger's fees ranged from $350 to at least $1,000. On November 10, 1865, after his return to Galveston, Ballinger noted in his diary that he had paid an uncle, Green Adams, $3,000, and had promised him at least $500 more for services connected with obtaining amnesty papers. As for himself, Ballinger indicated that he had netted, presumably after payment of the expenses of the trip to Washington, some $5,000 in cash, already collected; he expected further payments, including 300 acres of land, from two or three clients.[11]

George W. Paschal, Ballinger's associate in pardon brokerage, was a staunch Unionist. He had spent much of the war period in prison because of a clash with the Confederate provost marshal. While imprisoned, Paschal evidently had some freedom of action, for he had been able to prepare a manuscript that became famous as Paschal's *Digest of the Constitution and Laws of Texas.* After Provisional Governor Hamilton had taken over the government in Texas, Paschal had decided to go to Washington, D. C., in the hope of finding a publisher for his manuscript. Fortunately, Hamilton had appointed him agent for Texas, with the assignment to recover the indemnity bonds turned over to George W. White and John P. Chiles near the end of the war.[12]

Before leaving Austin, Paschal prepared a sheaf of amnesty applications and obtained Governor Hamilton's approval of them. These Paschal took with him to expedite personally in Washington. Throughout the period in which the amnesty policy was in effect, Paschal was quite active in this business. He made no apologies for charging for his work, which involved not only editing and presenting the applications but also following them up for approval. It is doubtful that Paschal earned any considerable sum of money in this activity, for he

11. *Ibid.,* entries of September 1, 20, November 10, 1865.
12. G. W. Paschal to E. M. Pease, January 14, February 26, October 11, 1866, in Graham-Pease Collection, Archives, Austin Public Library; Executive Record Book, No. 281, p. 38, Archives Division, Texas State Library; Amnesty Records, Texas, RG 940, Office of the Adjutant General, Box No. 54, National Archives; *Austin Republican,* May 19, June 5, 1869.

seems to have labored under financial difficulties during this time.

The present writer has not had access to special records relating to Paschal's accounts and cannot name his fee or fees—that is, whether he had one fee for all applicants or used a fee scale as Ballinger did. Paschal may have divided his fees with E. M. Pease—that is, with respect to the applications that Pease sent him. According to this practice, Pease prepared the applications in Austin, obtained Hamilton's approval, and sent them to Paschal in Washington.[13]

A close friend of E. M. Pease, James Masterson, also engaged in the amnesty business. His method of operation may be illustrated by a few examples. In handling the application of one John Kennedy, Masterson wrote ex-Governor Pease, who was close to Governor Hamilton, that the fee would be $250, and that Pease, if willing to cooperate in the enterprise, would receive half. No reply to this proposal from Pease has been found; but in another letter, Masterson referred to his previous communication, noting that Pease had not drawn the money deposited to his credit. In a short time, business picked up for Masterson and he engaged a partner. He then wrote to Pease that the fee, apparently the same for all clients, was to be $150, to be divided three ways. It appears that Pease accepted this arrangement. There was nothing legally or ethically wrong about charging fees in the business of securing amnesties, assuming that a legitimate service was rendered.[14]

It is interesting to consider Hamilton's attitude toward the applications for amnesty. Except for some twelve to fifteen, he approved all applications submitted to him. He made it a rule to disapprove the application of any graduate of West Point or the Naval Academy who had entered the service of

13. G. W. Paschal to E. M. Pease, January 14, February 26, October 11, 1866; January 21, February 21, July 22, 1867, in Graham-Pease Collection, Archives, Austin Public Library; James P. Hart, "George W. Paschal," *Texas Law Review,* XXVIII, p. 23.

14. James Masterson to E. M. Pease, July 31, September 21, October 5, 1865, in Graham-Pease Collection, Archives, Austin Public Library.

the Confederacy.[15] Since lawyers were quite active in seeking amnesties for their clients, Hamilton raised no objection to members of the bar earning reasonable fees for their services. At the same time, he did not want anyone to feel that he would be unduly influenced because an application had been prepared by a lawyer.[16]

Samuel A. Maverick, as a member of the subcommittee of the Confederate Committee of Public Safety, had helped engineer the surrender by General D. E. Twiggs of Federal military property in Texas. Maverick was among those who applied directly to Governor Hamilton for amnesty. In his letter, Maverick said that he was opposed to secession but that he simply lacked the force of character to withstand public pressure after the secession convention had acted. At the same time, he reminded Hamilton of his earlier opposition to nullification in South Carolina, and of leaving that State because of the agitation of the extremists and nullifiers. He went on to say that he had long been disturbed over the institution of slavery, and was glad to see it end. He asserted that he had not oppressed anyone during the war. Maverick concluded by saying that his attitude now was like that of an old friend who occasionally imbibed too freely and who, upon sobering up, remarked, "I am willing to be forgiven." Hamilton knew and respected Sam A. Maverick and enjoyed a good joke—especially of this kind. It is not at all surprising that the application was promptly and cordially approved.[17]

When the application for amnesty by Major Simeon Hart of El Paso came to Hamilton's desk, the Governor disapproved it. By this action, it is possible he did Hart an injustice. Hamilton believed the widespread reports that fortunes had

15. Amnesty Records, Texas, RG 940. See envelopes for the following: R. T. P. Allen, Box No. 51, Sam Bell Maxey, Box No. 52, H. C. McNeill, Felix H. Robinson, Thomas L. Rossen, Box No. 53, William Steele, Box No. 54—all in National Archives.

16. Hamilton's Proclamation of November 8, 1865, in Executive Record Book, No. 281 pp. 137-138, Archives Division, Texas State Library.

17. Samuel A. Maverick to Governor Hamilton, August 4, 1865, in Governors' Letters (Hamilton), Archives Division, Texas State Library; Amnesty Records, Texas, RG 940, envelope of Sam A. Maverick, Box No. 52, National Archives.

been made in cotton speculation in Texas during the war. As cotton agent for the Confederate War Department, Major Hart figured prominently in these reports. Hart was a resourceful man, however, and soon found influential supporters, not only in Texas but also in New York, and succeeded in getting amnesty direct from the President.[18]

George W. White, a prominent citizen of Austin, also gained amnesty over the opposition of Governor Hamilton.[19] The outcome was similar for E. B. Nichols, a leading business man of Galveston, who had been an agent of Governor Pendleton Murrah, Confederate Governor of Texas. Nichols represented Murrah in his efforts to get an accounting of the activities of the field workers of the Texas State Military Board, but Nichols never rendered a satisfactory report. Governor Hamilton flatly refused to approve Nichols' application and declared that he would continue to do so until Nichols cleared up his relations with the State. Yet, Ballinger, in consideration of the payment of $1,000 in gold, managed somehow without Hamilton's approval to secure amnesty for Nichols.[20] In another case, Governor Hamilton delayed presidential amnesty for Willard Richardson, editor and publisher of the Galveston *News*. In recommending that the application be rejected, the Governor wrote a strong indictment of "Ultraism" in bringing about secession, and of Richardson's rebellious, unreconstructed attitude following the war. In spite of Hamilton's opposition, however, Richardson eventually secured amnesty direct from President Johnson.[21]

While applications for presidential amnesty such as these

18. *Ibid.*, envelope for Simeon Hart, Box No. 52.
19. *Ibid.*, envelope of George W. White, Box No. 54; Governor Hamilton to President Andrew Johnson and Hugh McCulloch, Secretary of the U.S. Treasury, August 30, 1865, in Executive Record Book, No. 281, pp. 40-46; George W. Paschal to R. W. Taylor, Comptroller of the United States, September 1, 30, 1865, in Governors' Letters (Hamilton), Archives Division, Texas State Library.
20. Ballinger, Diary, entries of August 25, September 30, November 10, 1865; Amnesty Records, Texas, RG 940, Box No. 53, envelope of E. B. Nichols, National Archives; *Austin Republican*, May 12, 1869.
21. Amnesty Records, Texas, RG 940, Box No. 53, envelope of Willard Richardson, National Archives; Galveston *News*, April 28, July 22, August 8, 11, 1865, and next four years, *passim*.

were slowly being processed, the vast majority of voters in Texas were taking the amnesty oath, and their political leaders were preparing to assemble a constitutional convention. Such procedures took time, especially because of the near-break-down of all means for disseminating information. Many of the local newspapers had suspended publication; the mail service had almost ceased to function.[22]

In order to carry out the Reconstruction policy adopted to qualify voters, Secretary of State Seward announced that all State officials, as well as Army and Navy officers, would be authorized to administer the amnesty oaths. Governor Hamilton, however, soon realized that if these persons were to be the only ones so authorized, the work ahead would be seriously delayed; citizens living in the remote parts of the State would be greatly inconvenienced. Consequently, he issued a proclamation on August 19, 1865, announcing a plan for setting up amnesty boards in all counties. The board in each was to be composed of the chief justice and the two clerks (county and district), any two of whom would constitute a quorum. Each board was to prepare two lists, one to be retained by the county and the other to be sent to the Secretary of the State at Austin.[23]

In his Address to the People of Texas, September 11, 1865, Governor Hamilton made it clear that according to his instructions only those citizens known to be loyal were to vote for, or to serve as, delegates to the forthcoming constitutional convention.[24] Since progress in qualifying voters was slow, the call for the election of delegates was not issued until November 15, 1865. The Governor attempted, none too successfully, to prevent from voting anyone in the excluded classes who had

22. Governor Hamilton to President Andrew Johnson, August 30, 1865, in Executive Record Book, No. 281, p. 40, Archives Division, Texas State Library; W. M. Daily, Special Agent U.S. Post Office Department, to Governor Hamilton, November 15, 1865, in Governors' Letters (Hamilton), Archives Division, Texas State Library.
23. Executive Record Book, No. 281, pp. 28-31, Archives Division, Texas State Library; Austin *Republican*, August 25, 1865.
24. *Ibid.*, September 11, 1865; also Executive Record Book, No. 281, pp. 55-71, Archives Division, Texas State Library.

taken the oath of amnesty but had not received presidential amnesty.[25] On November 24, the Governor wrote President Johnson an explanation of the delays, with a request that Federal troops be kept in Texas.

President Johnson, in a telegram of December 1, 1865, approved the request for continued occupation by the troops.[26] As for the delay, one reason for it was that all who took the amnesty oath were required to accept all presidential proclamations concerning emancipation of the slaves. There were many persons who felt that Lincoln's Emancipation Proclamation was simply a military act—that it was not binding or constitutional. These persons hesitated to take the amnesty oath; they hoped for gradual emancipation, even compensation, for the loss of their slave properties.[27] Eventually, a sufficient number of Texans had been qualified for the election of delegates to proceed. Hamilton consequently designated January 8, 1866, for the election of delegates, and February 7 for the assembling of the convention.[28]

The number of delegates to which each district was entitled depended on its representation in the Legislature, and requirements for voting included taking the amnesty oath and meeting the voting requirements of the State as of February 1, 1861.[29] In the election, in spite of Governor Hamilton's proclamations, prominent leaders in the secession movement were chosen. When a quorum of the convention had arrived, these leaders assumed control of it.[30] They included extreme Seces-

25. Governor Hamilton's Proclamation of November 15, 1865, in *ibid.*, pp. 124-128.

26. Governor Hamilton to President Johnson, November 24, 1865, in *ibid.*, pp. 133-137; telegram of approval from the President, December 1, 1865, Governors' Letters (Hamilton), Archives Division, Texas State Library.

27. Warren A. Beck, "Lincoln and Negro Colonization in Central America," *Abraham Lincoln Quarterly*, VI, pp. 168-183.

28. Governor Hamilton's Proclamation of November 15, 1865, in Executive Record Book No. 28, pp. 124-128, Archives Division, Texas State Library.

29. *Journal of the Texas State Constitutional Convention Assembled at Austin, February 7, 1866* (printed at Southern Intelligencer Office, Austin, 1866), pp. 3-5. (Hereinafter cited as *Journal.*)

30. Hamilton's Proclamation of November 15, 1865, Executive Record Book No. 281, pp. 124-128, Archives Division, Texas State Library.

sionists—such as O. M. Roberts, H. R. Runnels, J. H. Parsons, and John Ireland.[31] Supported by George W. Paschal and other Unionists, the moderate E. M. Pease ran as a delegate from Travis County, but his opponent, John Hancock, was elected.[32] Hancock, it was charged by some, entered the race in the hope of being elected United States Senator later. As something of an opportunist, he became a "soft Unionist," that is, one who endeavored to lighten the burden falling on unreconstructed Secessionists. He outspokenly opposed giving the Negro the vote; he declared that he would be willing to do so when it was given to the mule.[33]

When the delegates assembled in Austin on February 7, 1866, J. W. Throckmorton suggested that the Secretary of State, James H. Bell, be requested to preside and accept the credentials of the delegates. The proposal was approved; sixty-three of the delegates were thus qualified, and they decided that a quorum was present.[34] Additional delegates arrived the next day; ultimately eighty-nine attended the convention. Throckmorton, elected president by the convention, was a logical choice, for he had voted against secession, yet had supported the Confederacy. It was hoped that he would be able to work for the conciliation of both extremes in the convention.[35]

Throckmorton, however, was in no respect neutral. A careful study of the work of the convention indicates that, in spite of his eloquent acceptance address in which he expressed the wish that all present would do their duty however distasteful it might be, he was clearly sympathetic to the Secessionists. The fact that a caucus of Secessionists and Conservatives later nominated him for Governor leaves no room to doubt his attitude.[36]

31. *Journal,* pp. 3-5.
32. T. H. Duval to E. M. Pease, November 18, 1865, in Graham-Pease Collection, Archives, Austin Public Library.
33. *Southern Intelligencer,* January 4, April 19, 1866.
34. *Journal,* p. 3.   35. *Ibid.,* pp. 5-6.
36. *Ibid.,* pp. 6-7; Ernest William Winkler (ed.), *Platforms of Political Parties in Texas* (Bulletin of the University of Texas, 1916, No. 53), p. 98

Following the election of officers and the organization of the convention for deliberations, Isaiah A. Paschal, dedicated Unionist from Bexar County, introduced the first important motion. He proposed that a committee be appointed to notify Governor Hamilton that the delegates were ready to take the loyalty oath. This proposal raised a furor which lasted most of the next two days. After their emotions had calmed somewhat, most of the delegates realized that their refusal to take an oath of loyalty would show them up in a most unfavorable light. Therefore, on February 10, a motion to reconsider Paschal's earlier motion passed; the original motion was then approved. Even so, the majority decided to take the oath *en masse.*[37]

A motion was then made and passed to invite Governor Hamilton to address the convention. Complying on the same day, he explained the nature of his appointment—what he considered his authority and duty to be. A few of his remarks were rather cutting and severe. In fact, several of his recommendations to the delegates were in the nature of demands. These included: (1) the disavowal of the right of secession and the acknowledgment that the Act of Secession of February 1, 1861, was null and void; (2) the recognition that slavery had ended; (3) the enactment of provisions for the protection of the Negroes and the establishment of guarantees for their rights to own property, enter into contracts, and sue and be sued; (4) the repudiation of the Civil War debt of Texas.

In regard to suffrage for Negroes, Hamilton explained that while some of them might be intellectually and otherwise qualified to exercise the privilege, he did not feel that all of them were qualified at this time to do so. He objected, however, to denying them the vote solely on the grounds of race or color. He insisted that requirements for voting should be based on legal principles and not on the accident of race or color. He made it clear that all of his recommendations were supported by instructions from President Johnson. Taken as a whole, in view of Hamilton's occasional inclination to make

37. *Journal,* pp. 11-14.

harsh remarks, the address was conciliatory.[38] Why then did the delegates fail to respond to his appeal? Why did they quibble over details and stall off action as long as possible?

Possibly one reason for the delay was the break that was developing between President Johnson and the Republican Radicals in Congress. Shortly after the Texas convention was organized, President Johnson delivered a bitter speech scoring Senator Charles Sumner and a number of other Radicals. Furthermore, the President vetoed the Civil Rights Act designed to guarantee the civil rights of the Negroes. This veto precipitated an open war with the Radicals. It is possible that the Secessionist delegates in the Texas convention hoped to profit from these developments in Washington.[39]

At the meeting in Austin, a month of wrangling resulted from the insistent demand of some of the Radical Unionist delegates, along with some other dissentient persons and groups, that the convention declare the Ordinance of Secession of February 1, 1861, not simply null and void as of then, but also to have been null and void *ab initio*—that is, from the beginning. The controversial question was finally settled with the adoption of a compromise resolution. The resolution recognized the supremacy of the Union, declared the Secession Ordinance of February 1, 1861, null and void, and renounced the right of secession heretofore claimed.[40]

From the viewpoint of Northern Radicals in Congress, the action of the Texas convention on the questions of ending slavery and affirming civil rights for the Negroes was unsatisfactory, and it doubtless encouraged them as they proceeded to formulate the Congressional Plan of Reconstruction. A proposal made by O. M. Roberts in the Texas body—to consider in cooperation with other Southern States the resettlement of the Negroes elsewhere—did not pour oil on

38. *Ibid.,* pp. 16-27; Executive Record Book No. 281, pp. 161-169, Archives Division, Texas State Library.
39. Morison and Commager, *Growth of the American Republic,* II, pp. 38-41.
40. *Southern Intelligencer,* January 11, February 22, 1866; *Journal,* February 12 through March 15, 1866, pp. 62, 148, 161-164, 183.

troubled waters either in Texas or in Washington.[41]

A voice of moderation now gained a hearing, but unfortunately it proved ineffectual. On August 11, 1865. John H. Reagan had appealed from his prison in Fort Warren to the people of Texas to act promptly in meeting the mild requirements of President Johnson and thus regain control of their State government. The appeal reached Governor Hamilton, who approved it warmly and gave it all the publicity possible. Reagan had been reading the leading newspapers of the North, and sensed the rising tide of Radicalism in Congress. He wanted to act quickly in allowing intelligent Negroes, possessed of some property, to vote. But the unreconstructed forces in the convention, instead of understanding and accepting the wisdom of the advice offered, turned on Reagan and vilified him.[42]

Ben C. Truman, correspondent of the New York *Times*, considered O. M. Roberts as rank a Secessionist as ever, declaring that "He is by all odds the most narrow-minded and contemptible rebel knave I have met in any of the conventions of the Southern States."[43] In twelve days of debate, Truman reported, the convention had not repealed the Ordinance of Secession, or declared it null and void.[44] One month after the convention had assembled, E. M. Pease remarked that it had accomplished "little or nothing."[45]

Yet, Governor Hamilton's suggestion that the Civil War debt of the State be repudiated received favorable treatment. It is true that a few delegates and certain editors and possibly some interested parties were angered. In spite of this

41. *Ibid.,* pp. 51, 81-91, 119, 368.
42.   John H. Reagan, "To the People of Texas," Fort Warren, Boston Harbor, August 11, 1865, in Walter Falvius McCaleb (ed.), *John H. Reagan, Memoirs, With Special Reference to Secession and the Civil War* (The Neale Publishing Company, New York, 1906), pp. 286-295; Ben Hamill Proctor, *Not Without Honor: The Life of John H. Reagan* (University of Texas Press, Austin, 1962), pp. 172, 176; Governor Hamilton to John H. Reagan, September 28, 1865, Executive Record Book, No. 281, pp. 83-84, Archives Division, Texas State Library.
43.   New York *Times,* March 5, 1866; March 11, 13, 18, 21, 22, 1866.
44.   *Ibid.,* March 11, 1866.
45.   E. M. Pease to his daughter Carrie, March 8, 1866, in Graham-Pease Collection, Archives, Austin Public Library.

fact, the entire debt of Texas created during the war was disavowed—on the ground that most of it was used to persecute Unionists.[46] The convention also gave much time to essentially legislative matters: the creation of corporations, proposals to divide the State, the General School Fund, the protection of individuals from the consequences of their acts during the war.[47] The convention adopted an ordinance designed in effect to exempt such persons from legal responsibility for their wartime acts.[48] This decision of the convention, along with its failure to carry out the spirit of Hamilton's other proposals, brought forth a terrific blast from the Governor. He declared that the convention had deliberately decided to protect certain reprehensible individuals from punishment. By its ordinance, he continued, the convention had condoned outrageous acts of robbery and cruel injustice to Unionists in Texas. He swore, with God's help, to ferret out and expose the criminals and their heinous crimes.[49]

In contrast, O. M. Roberts wrote his friend Judge T. J. Devine that he considered the decisions of the convention a victory for the Conservatives, with no pandering to Northern Radicals.[50] This assessment seems to have been justified. The convention refused to disavow the right of secession almost to the end of its sessions. It refused to ratify the Thirteenth Amendment and to legalize the claims of the Negroes for freedom. It was in no mood to recognize their fundamental civil rights.

46. *State Gazette,* February 15, 1866; *Journal.* pp. 46, 66, 116, 355-357.

47. *Ibid.,* pp. 46, 49, 54, 91, 135, 221.

48.   W. P. Ballinger to O. M. Roberts, March 9, 1866, in O. M. Roberts' Letters, Archives, University of Texas Library; An Ordinance Making Valid the Laws and Acts of Officers, etc., Sec. 5, p. 40, in *The Constitution of the State of Texas as Amended by the Delegates in the Convention Assembled, Austin, 1866* (printed at Southern Intelligencer Office, Austin, 1866); D. G. Wooten (ed.), *A Comprehensive History of Texas, 1685-1897* (2 Vols., W. G. Scarff, Dallas, 1898), Part III, p. 155.

49.   *Southern Intelligencer,* May 24, 1866.

50.   O. M. Roberts to T. J. Devine, April 2, 1866, in Appendix of Mary Owen Meredith, "The Life and Work of Thomas Jefferson Devine" (M.A. thesis, University of Texas, 1930).

In concluding its work, the Constitutional Convention of 1866 provided for a popular vote to determine whether the new constitution would be adopted, and for an election to choose local and State officials. At the same time, the convention took no action with regard to a Congressional election, making it appear, on the surface at least, that the delegates were more concerned with winning control of local and State offices than in regaining representation in the National Congress. The general elections were to be in June.[51] Party activists decided to use caucuses for nominating their candidates.

A coalition of Secessionists—including O. M. Roberts, J. W. Henderson, H. R. Runnels, and J. H. Parsons—along with moderates going under the name of the Conservative Union Party, nominated J. W. Throckmorton for Governor and George W. Jones for Lieutenant Governor.[52] Another group of voters calling themselves the Union Party selected E. M. Pease as their candidate for Governor and A. H. Latimer for Lieutenant Governor.[53] A. J. Hamilton was the acknowledged leader of the Unionists in Texas, but he had no desire at this time to run for Governor. He felt that Pease was the wisest choice of those who shared his views.[54]

From the outset, the election campaign was filled with bitterness and recriminations. Hamilton, in effect, had set the tone of the campaign in making his severe attack on the delegates in the constitutional convention who wished to protect the Secessionists from the consequences of their acts during the war. In addition, a report was circulated to the effect that Hamilton had stated publicly his belief that in point of honor, integrity, and patriotism, the Negroes were immeasurably superior to the whites. The report was false. Although when he was under emotional stress, Hamilton could, and

51. *Southern Intelligencer,* April 12, 19, 1866; *Journal,* p. 344.
52. Winkler, *Platforms of Political Parties in Texas,* p. 98; *Southern Intelligencer,* April 19, 1866.
53. *Ibid.,* April 19, 1866; Winkler, *Platforms of Political Parties in Texas,* p. 95.
54. *Southern Intelligencer,* June 7, 1866; Throckmorton to B. H. Epperson, April 18, 25, 1866, in Epperson Papers, Archives, University of Texas Library.

occasionally did, make rash statements, his whole life belied any such statement as the one attributed to him.

Another rumor, which related to the early life of Hamilton, originated in a Nashville, Tennessee, newspaper. Clipped and circulated over Texas during the campaign, it claimed that Hamilton had robbed his merchant employer and fled from Alabama to Texas, where he had earned the reputation of being an unprincipled pettifogger. The *Southern Intelligencer* denounced this account as untrue, a fact known to every responsible editor and every reputable lawyer in Texas.[55]

Hamilton's cutting remarks and the false stories concerning him that were circulated throughout Texas doubtless had an adverse effect on the Unionist cause in the election. But the majority for Throckmorton, the opposing candidate, was so large that the aspersions against Hamilton could not have been a deciding factor.[56] The election result—49,277 for Throckmorton and 12,168 for Pease[57]—together with the failure of the constitutional convention to carry out the recommendations for Reconstruction in Texas, undoubtedly strengthened the position of the Radicals in Congress. For a few weeks it was uncertain whether Throckmorton and the Legislature would be permitted to take office. In fact, not until July 28, 1866, did Secretary of State William H. Seward authorize the Legislature to assemble and Throckmorton to be inaugurated as Governor.[58]

It became clear during the sessions of the constitutional convention that the Radicals in the North had come to regard President Johnson as no longer a godsend striving to make treason odious, but as an obstruction to the enactment of a righteous program. Perhaps some political leaders in Texas had concluded that the differences now developing between

55. *Southern Intelligencer,* May 24, 1866.
56. *Ibid.,* April-May, 1866; *State Gazette,* April-May, 1866.
57. *Journal of the House of Representatives of the Eleventh Legislature* (State Gazette Office, Printers, Austin, 1866), pp. 11-16.
58. Telegrams from Secretary of State Seward to James H. Bell, Secretary of State of Texas, in Executive Record Book No. 281, pp. 196, 197, 198-227, 230, Archives Division, Texas State Library.

the President and the Radicals could be used to their advantage. But as the rift widened and deepened, Radical Republicans in Texas—men like William Alexander—began to fear that a call from President Johnson would cause the unreconstructed rebels to rally, and that another bloody civil war would be precipitated.[59] This idea may sound fantastic to most Texans today; it is nevertheless disturbing to read many letters of that time, shot through and through as they were with agitation and fear. Such letters asserted that Congress must act promptly with vigor, otherwise all Union people must leave Texas.[60]

Hamilton himself was deeply concerned, as shown by his speeches in Texas during the election campaign in the spring of 1866. He left Austin on May 31 to go to Washington, D. C., and at this time he may have already decided to join the Radicals.[61] For the next three years, he became involved in a number of activities. He espoused the causes of Radical Republicanism; he promoted the building of railroads; he served as an associate justice on the Texas Supreme Court and as a delegate to the Reconstruction convention in Texas; he became a candidate for Governor. The chapters that follow deal with these activities in the order mentioned.

59. William Alexander to E. M. Pease, July 17-18, September 6, November 8, 26, 1866; January 4, 1867, in Graham-Pease Collection, Archives, Austin Public Library.

60. Alexander's letters above; T. H. Duval to E. M. Pease, August 9, 1866; E. J. Davis to E. M. Pease, July 14, 1866; John L. Haynes to E. M. Pease, October 1, 4, November 27-30, 1866—all in Graham-Pease Collection, Archives, Austin Public Library.

61. *Southern Intelligencer,* June 7, 1866; *State Gazette,* April 28, 1866.

CHAPTER VII

Radical Republican and Railroad Promoter

WITHIN A YEAR after Lincoln's assassination, President Johnson was confronted by the bitter opposition of the Radicals in Congress—widening and deepening the breach that had developed between him and them. Conservative supporters of the President, in order to give him effective backing, assembled a convention in Philadelphia, August, 14, 1866. A strong delegation from Texas attended.[1]

Henry J. Raymond, editor and publisher of the New York *Times,* supported the convention. Raymond wrote many editorials in praise of the delegates chosen; in the end, he endorsed the deliberations of the convention and its final results.[2] On the other hand, the editor and publisher of the New York *Tribune,* Horace Greeley, viewed the convention with suspicion. He regarded some of the delegates as disloyal Northern "Copperheads" and unrepentant Southern rebels; he charged that the purpose of the convention was to sacrifice the safety of the Southern Unionists and the political rights of the freedmen.[3] Raymond and the *Times,* it is clear, hoped to maintain the integrity of the Union Party that had elected Lincoln in 1864, and to strengthen the position of President Johnson by attracting the support of the Southern Conservatives.[4]

Following the adjournment of the convention, two acts of President Johnson brought about sharp reaction from the

1. New York *Times,* July 2, August 14, 1866; New York *Tribune,* August 13, 1866.
2. New York *Times,* July 6, 17, 19, 23, 31; August 1, 2, 14, 17, 1866.
3. *Ibid.,* August 21, 29, 30, 1866; New York *Tribune,* August 17, September 1, 1866.
4. *Ibid.,* over same period, especially August 13, 1866; New York *Times,* August 18, 1866.

Radicals: his proclamation for the reestablishment of civil government in the South and his so-called "Swing Around the Circle" speaking tour. Johnson made the tour in the hope of gaining a working majority in Congress to support him. But his plan to control the course of events failed. To checkmate his efforts, a convention of Southern Loyalists assembled in Philadelphia, September 3, 1866. A. J. Hamilton was one of the leaders who had issued the call for the convention. He had by now concluded that the restoration of Texas and the South could be achieved only by following the Radical course.[5]

As to this convention, the positions of Raymond of the *Times* and Greeley of the *Tribune* were reversed. Raymond, suspicious of its objectives, attempted to discredit its leaders, especially Hamilton and Greeley. He charged that the convention had for its chief purpose insistence on Negro suffrage as a requirement for Reconstruction. Greeley, on the contrary, viewed the convention as a constructive effort to implement Lincoln's policies, from which his successor was veering.[6] What caused Hamilton to break with President Johnson and to ally with the Radicals in Congress? The answer seems to be that Hamilton had come to believe that the safeguards essential for the Southern Unionists and the freedmen could be attained only by Congressional Reconstruction. And once Hamilton had joined the Radicals, he was to go all the way in accepting and supporting their plans. In addition to Hamilton, the Unionists of Texas sent to the convention delegates known as "out-and-out Radicals." That the Texas group was influential is shown by the fact that Hamilton was one of the opening speakers and that he spoke often.

Hamilton, moreover, was named chairman of the Committee on Resolutions; also as a member of the committee which followed President Johnson in his Swing Around the Circle. Members of the latter committee were charged with replying to the President as he toured the country in defense

5. *Ibid.*, August 21, 31, 1866.
6. See both papers, for issues of September 1-18, 1866.

of his policies.[7] Hamilton delivered a prepared address in Tremont Temple, Boston, on December 3, 1866, supporting Congressional Reconstruction; this fact demonstrates his commitment to the Radical program, including suffrage for the Negro and military rule in the South.[8] In view of Hamilton's well-known convictions, it is possible that he played a leading role in formulating the policy of thoroughgoing Reconstruction.

After his tenure as Provisional Governor ended, on August 9, 1866, Hamilton found himself in a precarious position. His alignment with the Radicals had left him without hope of further presidential patronage; there remained to him only such favors as friendly members of Congress or friendly administrative officials might offer him. Normally, he might have returned to the practice of law, but according to his own account he had almost entirely neglected his profession for the past eight years.[9] He had become in effect a politician without a base of operations and a lawyer without clients.

Lacking a steady income and with no regular duties, Hamilton inevitably fell into idleness and debt. George W. Paschal graphically described Hamilton's plight in a letter to S. M. Swenson, February 21, 1867, appealing for help for the fallen giant. After pointing out the great services that Hamilton had rendered Texas and the nation, Paschal noted that the former Governor was in debt and was getting in deeper.

7. New York *Tribune*, September 3, 4, 6, 8, 1866; New York *Times*, August 31, September 3, 4, 6, 8, 1866.

8. Andrew Jackson Hamilton, *An Address on "Suffrage and Reconstruction," the Duty of the People, the President and Congress: Delivered at the Invitation of the Impartial-Suffrage League, at Tremont Temple in Boston, December 3, 1866* (Impartial-Suffrage League, 1866), in Austin Public Library; John L. Haynes' Tribute to A. J. Hamilton, in *Evening Ranchero*, Brownsville, Texas, April 22, 1875.

9. Walter Prescott Webb and H. Bailey Carroll (eds.), *The Handbook of Texas* (2 vols., Texas State Historical Association, Austin, 1952), I, p. 759; A. J. Hamilton to E. M. Pease October 28, 1867; George W. Paschal to E. M. Pease, January 21, 23, 26, 1867—all in Graham-Pease Collection, Archives, Austin Public Library; Bar and Motion Dockets, 1865-1872, Office of the District Clerk, Travis County, Texas; *Southern Intelligencer*, April 11, 1867.

He had a family to support and children to educate, but he was wasting his talents and drinking to excess. Paschal went on to say that if he were financially able, he would pay off Hamilton's debts, after getting him to take a pledge to stop drinking. The immediate outcome of this correspondence is uncertain. It is known, however, that Swenson sent Paschal's appeal to E. M. Pease, for it was found in his letter files.[10]

Within a few months of Paschal's appeal, news of Hamilton's situation became known in Washington; then no less a personage than Salmon P. Chase, Chief Justice of the United States, came to his aid. As Chief Justice, Chase was authorized to name the registers in bankruptcy in the Federal judiciary located in all parts of the country. Fortunately for Hamilton, there was a vacancy at Brookhaven, Mississippi, to which Chase appointed him. This appointment was indeed an unexpected piece of good luck for Hamilton, putting him on his feet financially and enabling him to provide for his family adequately. In this new environment, encouraged by friends and family, Hamilton rapidly regained his confidence and composure.[11]

Now happy in his renewed ability to provide for his family's needs, Hamilton settled his wife and children not in Brookhaven but in New Orleans, some eighty miles to the south. The superior educational advantages in the Louisiana metropolis led to this decision. But unfortunately at this time, New Orleans was plagued with yellow fever. Unexpectedly—and as a crushing blow to the Hamiltons—their younger son John contracted the disease and died. The loss was especially poignant to Hamilton, who declared that the boy had possessed all the virtues and none of the vices of his father.[12]

10. George W. Paschal to E. M. Pease, February 21, 1867, in Graham-Pease Collection, Archives, Austin Public Library.
11. E. M. Pease, New Orleans, June 21, 1867, to Julie Pease, in *ibid.;* Revised *Statutes of the United States Passed at the First Session of the 40th Congress, 1873-1874* (Government Printing Office, Washington, D. C., 1874), Sec. 4993, p. 972.
12. *Flake's Bulletin,* November 14, 1868; May 5, 1869; A. J. Hamilton to M. C. Hamilton, September 22, 1867; A. J. Hamilton to Mary Hamilton Mills, October 7, 1867—both in A. J. Hamilton Papers, Archives, University of Texas Library.

Shortly before John's death, or soon afterwards, the Hamilton family moved to Brookhaven and remained there until Hamilton resigned his office of Register of Bankruptcy. Soon, he was ready to resume his more active career in politics.

Late in the fall of 1867 Hamilton returned to Texas, becoming active again in governmental affairs. First, he accepted appointment as Associate Justice of the State Supreme Court, on which he served with distinction for some time, as will appear in the following chapter. Next, without abandoning his judicial duties, he played a leading role in the Texas constitutional convention of 1868, the so-called Reconstruction Convention, a subject also to be covered in the next chapter.[13] During the same year, he was chosen a delegate to the Republican presidential nominating convention, controlled by the Radicals, that nominated General U. S. Grant for President. At that convention Hamilton was chosen a member of the National Executive Committee and of the Committee on Platform and Resolutions.[14]

Because Hamilton had vigorously supported Grant, the Texan for several months stood in the favor of both the new President and the Radical leaders of Congress. All the while, though, an important change was taking place in Hamilton's attitude on Reconstruction. In rethinking his position, he ultimately found that he could not be a true Radical. By instinct and by reason, he was a Moderate—the fact became increasingly clear during the Texas Reconstruction Convention. But his shift of position had serious implications: as soon as the Radical leaders in Grant's cabinet and in Congress became aware of the change in his views, they turned against him. His influence with the Radicals declined to the point that they deserted him in the race for Governor, throwing their support to E. J. Davis.[15]

13. A. J. Hamilton to E. M. Pease, October 28, 1867, in Graham-Pease Collection, Archives, Austin Public Library; *Journal of the Reconstruction Convention Which Met at Austin, Texas, June 1, A.D., 1868* (Tracy, Siemering & Co., Printers, Austin, 1870), *passim.*
14. *Flake's Bulletin,* May 20, 27, 1868; Austin *Republican,* June 3, 1868.
15. *Ibid.,* April 9, May 8, 1869; *Flake's Bulletin,* October 20, 1869.

This rebuff, as matters turned out, served only to arouse Hamilton's fighting spirit. The President's opponents—now including Hamilton—were prompted by the graft and scandals of Grant's first term to organize in protest. They formed the Liberal Republican Party, in which Hamilton's friend and admirer Horace Greeley played a prominent part. When their convention met in Cincinnati during May, 1872, Hamilton functioned as leader of the Texas delegation. The convention nominated Greeley as the standard bearer of the Liberal Republicans, and he soon received the endorsement of the Democrats. The nominee met Hamilton's test of moderation, since Greeley had come out for general amnesty. As could have been expected, Hamilton gave the Liberal Republican-Democratic candidate his full support.

In 1871, Hamilton had accompanied Greeley on a short speaking tour in Texas.[16] During the presidential campaign of 1872, Hamilton made a number of speeches in behalf of the Liberal movement and its leader.[17] It was rumored that Hamilton desired appointment to the Federal bench in Texas, and that his support of Greeley was motivated by personal ambition.[18] If Greeley had won, it is reasonably certain that Hamilton would have received some such reward. Nevertheless, the Texan conscientiously believed that the trend toward Radicalism must be arrested in the interest of the people and that Greeley, if elected, could accomplish this purpose.

While carrying the weight of the activities just described, Hamilton became deeply interested in another challenging subject. Clearly, a man of remarkable energy and drive, he became involved in an activity to which he had already given some attention—the promotion of railroads. He spent much

16. Samuel Eliot Morison and Henry Steele Commager, *The Growth of the American Republic* (2 vols., Oxford University Press, New York, 1950), II, pp. 69-71; Paul Casdorph, *A History of the Republican Party in Texas, 1865-1965* (Pemberton Press, Austin, 1965), p. 22; Houston *Telegraph*, May 23, 1871.

17. *Ibid.*, May 28, June 26, 1872; *State Gazette*, June 7, August 28, October 21, 23, 28, 1872.

18. San Antonio *Herald*, November 5, 1872; *State Gazette*, April 11, 1870.

time dealing with various aspects of railroad building. First, some time after the end of the war, he turned his attention to the tangled affairs of the Memphis, El Paso and Pacific Railroad. The Legislature of Texas first chartered this corporation on February 4, 1853,[19] and rechartered it on February 4, 1856.[20] The railroad was to be built from a point on the Red River, the eastern boundary of Texas, to a point near El Paso. The Legislature had granted the company a subsidy of sixteen sections of land for each mile of construction. Public lands were reserved on both sides of the right-of-way. The land subsidy was the most valuable asset of the Memphis, El Paso and Pacific.[21] The railroad project and the land that went with it provoked some unfavorable reactions. In the Reconstruction Convention, a number of delegates manifested hostility. As a result, a majority in the convention decided that the land grant of the Memphis, El Paso and Pacific should be opened to settlement. The majority further sought to forfeit all lands not already alienated by the company. The *Journal* of the convention does not show clearly how Hamilton voted on the various motions affecting the railroad, although he had earlier supported the policy of land grants for an international railroad. The Constitution of 1869, nevertheless, forbade land subsidies for railroad construction in Texas.[22]

As a result of the convention's decision, the unalienated land that had been appropriated to the Memphis, El Paso and Pacific Railroad was in effect forfeited when E. J. Davis became Governor of Texas in 1870. He and his Commissioner of the General Land Office, Jacob Kuechler, attempted to encourage settlement on the reserved lands along the right-of-way. In the meantime, the railroad company had been forced into receivership. In the face of the actions of Governor Davis, the receiver, John A. C. Gray, resorted to

19. H. P. N. Gammel (comp.), *Laws of Texas* (10 vols., Austin, 1898), III, p. 1433.

20. *Ibid.,* IV, p. 377.   21. *Ibid.,* IV, pp. 7, 377.

22. *Journal of the Reconstruction Convention, 1868-69, op. cit.,* 1st Sess., pp. 20, 66-71, 107, 229-332, 418, 429, 828; 2nd Sess., pp. 166, 170; Gammel, *Laws of Texas,* VI, p. 57, VII, p. 419.

the Federal courts. He applied to the judge of the Western Judicial District of Texas for an injunction to prevent the Governor and the Land Commissioner from infringing on the land reservation of the railroad company. Counsel for the beleaguered enterprise, including A. J. Hamilton, succeeded in obtaining the injunction they had sought.[23]

While these developments were taking place, pressure was building up for the Twelfth Legislature to grant charters and subsidies to other railroads. Two leading promoters, John C. Fremont and Marshall Roberts of New York, had organized the Southern Transcontinental Railway Company. They and the stockholders of the Southern Pacific Railroad— not the present road of that name—had applied to the Twelfth Legislature for charters. The Legislature not only acted favorably on the charters; it went much further. It gave the companies authority to acquire the assets of the Memphis, El Paso and Pacific Railroad; it also voted a subsidy of $6,000,000 in the form of 30-year State bonds bearing interest at 8 per cent.[24]

The transaction was so unusual, and so obviously prejudicial to the interests of the State, that Hamilton became convinced that wholesale bribery must have been used in obtaining the concessions from the Legislature. On the basis of evidence that he acquired, he also concluded that James H. Bell, Secretary of State during Hamilton's tenure as Provi-

23. J. J. Bowen, "The Texas and Pacific Railway Company Reservation and Land Grant" (An Address Presented to the Texas Surveyors Association Short Course, October 9, 1962, MS.), pp. 12-14; Circuit Court of the United States for the Western District of Texas. *In Equity.* John A. C. Gray, A Citizen of New York, Receiver of the Memphis, El Paso, and Pacific Railroad Company, Complainant (and Represented by A. J. Hamilton, E. M. Pease, and E. B. Turner, as Counsel) and Edmund J. Davis, Governor of Texas, and Jacob Kuechler, Commissioner of the General Land Office of Texas, Both Citizens of Texas, Defendants. Counsel for Defendants: Ballinger, Jack & Mott, Solicitors for Defendants. Justice Joseph P. Bradley, Associate Justice of the U. S. Supreme Court, Deciding in favor of the Complainant, and Enjoining Defendants (July 6, 1870). Tract published by Gray & Davenport, New York City, in Eugene Campbell Barker Texas History Center, University of Texas Library; 16 Wall (US), 203.

24. *House Journal,* Twelfth Legislature, p. 753; *Handbook of Texas,* II, pp. 643, 767.

sional Governor and a former member of the State Supreme Court, had made the illegal arrangements with members of the Legislature. In referring to the matter later, Hamilton remarked somewhat cynically that according to rumors there was some doubt that the "virtuous" legislators sponsoring the project had received any money from the "Puritan" capitalists. Hamilton readily admitted that he had been interested in the promotion of the Memphis, El Paso and Pacific Railroad for some time—as early as the spring of 1869—and that he had worked to secure a congressional land grant for it. But he denied taking part directly or indirectly in the disgraceful scramble of the railroad companies for subsidies during the meetings of the Twelfth Legislature.[25]

While unreservedly opposing the unethical maneuvers centering around the Twelfth Legislature (1870-71), Hamilton took an active part in another, more commendable, railroad promotion. He was prominent among the leaders of Austin who sought to induce the Houston and Texas Central Railroad to enter the city in 1871. This endeavor called for action by both the Twelfth Legislature and the City of Austin. The railroad management insisted that as a basic condition the Legislature should specifically recognize as valid the payment of $156,000 which the railroad had made during the Civil War to the Confederate Government of Texas in satisfaction of loans made to it by the State. The railroad executives also wanted from the City of Austin liberal grants of land for a right-of-way, a station, and yards. Apparently all of these demands were met, for the railroad entered Austin in December, 1871. It is likely that Hamilton did not negotiate with the Legislature but confined his activities to those aspects of the transaction that concerned the City of Austin.[26]

Although Hamilton had opposed the manner in which the

25. A. J. Hamilton to W. W. Mills, June 21, 1871; A. J. Hamilton to A. H. Longley, August 6, 1870. Editor Longley commented on this letter in the *Austin Republican,* July 27, and August 10, 1870; *Flake's Bulletin,* April 17, 1869; also see Austin *Republican,* June 30, 1869.
26. *Ibid.,* May 11, September 7, 1870; *Daily State Journal,* May 4, 6, 18, 1870; Gammel, *Laws of Texas,* VI, pp. 843-848.

Transcontinental and the Southern Pacific railroads had ma-
neuvered in the Twelfth Legislature, once their charters were
granted he helped to organize both of them, becoming a director in each company. One provision in the charter of the
Southern Trans-Continental Railway Company authorized
the company to purchase the franchises and other assets of
the Memphis, El Paso and Pacific Railroad.[27] In the meantime, Congress granted a charter of incorporation to the Texas
and Pacific Railway Company on March 3, 1871, authorizing
it to take over all assets of the Southern Trans-Continental
and the Southern Pacific railroads. A. J. Hamilton was one
of incorporators of Texas and Pacific Railway Company, and
he lobbied in Congress for the approval of its charter. The
directors of the Texas and Pacific, by affecting the mergers
contemplated, established one of the most important railroads
in the nation.[28]

In discussing his connection with the Texas and Pacific,
Hamilton was not slow in pointing out the value of his services to the company. These, he concluded, merited a large
fee, which he fully expected to receive. His labors in behalf
of the Texas and Pacific were the culmination of his efforts
in promoting the construction of railroads.[29]

Besides these railroad promotions, Hamilton in his late
fifties served as a member of the State Supreme Court and
a delegate to the Texas Reconstruction Convention. The
following chapter takes up in detail these two phases of his
career.

27. *State Gazette*, April 7, 1871; *The Texas New Yorker* (New York),
February, 1871, p. 85; *ibid.*, I, April, 1871, p. 118.

28. Gammel, *Laws of Texas*, VI, pp. 40-43, 542; *House Journal, Twelfth
Legislature*, pp. 753, 1705; *United States Statutes at Large*, XVI, p. 673.

29. A. J. Hamilton to W. W. Mills, June 21, 1871, A. J. Hamilton Papers,
Archives, University of Texas Library.

CHAPTER VIII

Associate Justice - Convention Delegate

WHILE ENGAGED in the activities described in the preceding chapter, A. J. Hamilton served for a time as a member of one of the three Reconstruction supreme courts that functioned in Texas between 1866 and 1873.[1] The members of the first Reconstruction Court were chosen by the voters in the election of 1866 at the time they chose J. W. Throckmorton as Governor. After one year of service, both he and they were removed by the military authorities as an "impediment to Reconstruction."[2] Now in control of the government of Texas, these authorities proceeded to set up the so-called "Military Supreme Court,"[3] to which A. J. Hamilton was appointed as an associate justice, December 10, 1867. Hamilton served in this capacity until he resigned, a little less than two years later, October 1, 1869.[4]

During Hamilton's incumbency, the Military Supreme Court was obliged to take up and decide many cases that had been "sleeping" on the dockets of the district courts during the war. A number of these involved difficult, even explosive, issues: the sale of slaves, labor contracts relating to slaves, sequestrations of enemy property, payments of obligations in Confederate currency, the administration of estates, and the like. There was a general feeling among Radicals, north and south, that all legislative and administrative acts of the South during secession, including secession itself, were null and void. The Military Court met these issues squarely, and with com-

1. James R. Norvell, "The Reconstruction Courts of Texas, 1867-1873," *Southwestern Historical Quarterly*, LXII, pp. 143-145, 148.
2. *Ibid.*, p. 144; General Phil Sheridan, Special Orders, No. 105, New Orleans, July 30, 1867, in Executive Record Book, No. 84, p. 365, Archives Division, Texas State Library.
3. Election Register No. 263, pp. 36-37, Archives Division, Texas State Library.
4. *Ibid.*, No. 264, *loc. cit.*

mendable restraint. It promptly ruled as legal and binding all acts not in support of the war, unless they were clearly unconstitutional.

As a member of the Court, Justice Hamilton was not as active or as productive in writing opinions as the other justices—Morrill, Lindsay, and Coldwell. One reason was that during part of his tenure he served also as a delegate to the Constitutional Convention of 1868-1869, and his activity in this capacity undoubtedly limited his judicial labors. Yet one observer of Hamilton's tenure on the Court stated that his opinions, though comparatively few, were "noted for learning, dignity, and force."

While Hamilton's time on the Court was limited, he nevertheless rendered Texas a noteworthy service in writing several landmark opinions. Outstanding among these were the series known as "the Sequestration Cases": *Luter v. Hunter* (30 Tex. 688), *Canfield v. Hunter* (30 Tex. 712), and *Culbreath v. Hunter* (30 Tex. 713). These cases arose as a result of laws enacted by the Confederate Congress. These Sequestration Acts provided for seizure by the Confederate Government of the properties belonging to enemy aliens and to citizens leaving Southern jurisdiction during the war. In Texas, the Sequestration Cases involved judgments in favor of a property owner whose holdings had been sequestrated under the acts, the judgments being appealed to the Military Court.

The respondent in the Sequestration Cases, William L. Hunter, was a man of property in Texas who had left the State shortly after secession. On leaving, he had left property in the care af E. Luter as his agent. The liquid assets entrusted to Luter included a promissory note for $100, due on March 19, 1861, from Luter himself. In keeping with the provisions of the Sequestration Acts, Luter had been persuaded to furnish Confederate officials with a list of all properties and assets he held for Hunter.

For the purpose of taking over Hunter's assets from Luter, the Confederate district judge had then issued a garnishment.

Following this court's pronouncement of sequestration order-
ing Luter to turn over Hunter's property to a Confederate
receiver, Luter had done so. Asked subsequently by the court
whether he owed Hunter any personal debt, Luter had answer-
ed that he owed on the promissory note for $100, with accrued
interest. The court had thereupon entered a judgment in that
amount against Luter, who satisfied it without protest. He
had paid the amount to an official receiver in Confederate
treasury notes, accepted at their face value.

Hunter had brought suit to recover on the promissory note
in question upon his return to Texas after the war was over.
Luter had offered in his own defense the Stay Laws, the Stat-
ute of Limitations, and the fact that he had paid the note
by remittance into the Confederate Treasury. On Hunter's
winning the suit against him in the lower court, Luter had
appealed to the Military Supreme Court, hence *Luter v.
Hunter*.

In analyzing the case in the Court opinion, Hamilton went
into considerable detail, but the salient points can be sum-
marized as follows:

(1)   The Sequestration Acts were null and void: the Confederacy had functioned as a government in rebellion, and
without legal capacity; any acts in aid of the rebellion, whether
of the Confederate Congress or courts, or of its State legislatures or courts, were illegal, null and void. (2)   The Stay
Laws were unconstitutional in that they conflicted with Article I, Section 10, of the Constitution of the United States.
One provision of Section 10 forbids any State to enact "any
law impairing the obligation of contracts." (Hamilton further
pointed out that the Stay Laws violated the Texas Constitution.)   (3)   Payment into the Confederate Treasury could
not be held to have satisfied a debt owed to an individual—
to honor such repayment would in effect constitute recognition of the Confederate States of America as a legal government, a conclusion unacceptable on its face.

The other Sequestration Cases *Canfield v. Hunter* and

Culbreath v. Hunter, were analogous. The brief opinions state the issues and the decisions to be the same. Referring to these cases, one observer remarked, "It would have been well indeed if the doctrine enunciated in these cases had been accepted by the dominant party [Republican]: the hostility of the heart would have ended with the hostility of the sword."[5]

One of Hamilton's dissents from the Military Court majority calls for special mention. *Hall v. Keese* (31 Tex. 504) involved the question: When did slavery cease to exist in Texas? Chief Justice Morrill, speaking for the majority of the Court, had decided that all contracts relating to the sale of slaves, or the labor of slaves, entered into before June 19, 1865, could be enforced. This date was that of General Gordon Granger's Proclamation of General Orders, No. 3. Justice Hamilton, joined by Justice Coldwell, delivered a strong and eloquent dissent. Hamilton's dissent argued that the Emancipation Proclamation of January 1, 1863, had specifically annulled the status of the Negro as property in the belligerent states. Therefore, no subsequent contracts disposing of Negroes as property should be upheld. The majority of the Court, however, acted in a more realistic and practical manner: They held to the later date—that of the Proclamation of General Gordon, June 19, 1865—as ending the legality of slavery in Texas.

Several other opinions of Hamilton's which dealt with a variety of issues show the scope of his judicial activities. *Secrest v. Jones* (30 Tex. 569) illustrates the intention of the Military Court, with Hamilton as its spokesman, to maintain the integrity of the judicial system of Texas. This integrity— and specifically the principle of *res judicata*—had to prevail in spite of the policies of Reconstruction. The case, which concerned the settlement of Secrest's estate, had been decided, in the district court, against the claims of his executors. On appeal in 1858, the Texas Supreme Court had let the deci-

5. Lewis E. Daniell, *Personnel of the Texas State Government, Sketches of Representative Men of Texas* (Maverick Printing House, San Antonio, 1942), p. 421; James D. Lynch, *The Bench and Bar of Texas* (Nixon-Jones Printing Co., St. Louis, 1885), p. 104.

sion of the lower court stand. The Military Court, on a rehearing and speaking through Justice Hamilton, sustained the previous decisions, thus placing its authority behind due process of law in the State.

A later case, *Donley v. Tindall* (32 Tex. 43), turned on the legality of an obligation that originated during the days of the Confederacy. The appeal came up from a district court in a suit aimed to collect on a note for $5,000. The note, signed by Tindall, the defendant, had been executed in favor of J. M. Brittain, with promise to pay on or before December 25, 1864. Donley, the plaintiff, had acquired the note in due course, but the district court had denied him relief on the ground that the suit involved an illegal contract. Donley had then appealed to the Military Court. Justice Hamilton, giving the opinion of the Court, held that the contract was illegal, since it presumed that payment would be made in Confederate money. He pointed out that the enforcement of such a contract would in effect recognize the legality of the rebellion against the Union. The Military Court accordingly affirmed the decision of the lower court holding the note to be invalid.

In *Magee v. Chadoin* (30 Tex. 644), another opinion which Justice Hamilton wrote, the Court demonstrated its conservative concept of property rights. Regardless of the war and Reconstruction, the Court intended to recognize property rights and to protect them. The case had come up over the title of Chadoin, an early settler in Texas, to a league of land, a portion of which other persons had appropriated for their own use. To protect his interests, Chadoin had sued in the district court and obtained an order for the trespassers to vacate his land. When the case came up on appeal, Hamilton acting for the majority of the Court, presented an exhaustive review and analysis of the issues involved. The decision confirmed Chadoin's title unequivocally.

In *Greer v. The State* (31 Tex. 129), the Court, again speaking through Justice Hamilton, showed that it intended to protect scrupulously the procedural rights of citizens during the period of Reconstruction. Greer, charged with theft of a watch, had been convicted. He appealed to the Military Court on the ground that law officers by means of threats had caused him to give evidence against himself. As a result of their threats, he had shown them where he had concealed the watch. Justice Hamilton, invoking the Code of Criminal Procedure, ruled on the question of involuntary confessions obtained from accused persons while they were in custody. He concluded that such forced confessions and the evidence supporting them could not be used against the accused. The conviction of Greer was annulled.

Two other opinions that Hamilton wrote manifested the intention of the majority of the Court to maintain the integrity of the legal system of Texas during the trying period of Reconstruction. In *Vincent v. Rather* (31 Tex. 77), Hamilton's decision upheld the rights of a bailor in a routine commercial transaction. In *Hicklin v. The State* (31 Tex. 492), Hamilton insisted that an appeal in a criminal case entailed the submission of supporting evidence as required by law.

One other opinion which Hamilton wrote deserves attention—*Hart v. Mills* (31 Tex. 513). The case grew out of a celebrated dispute that originated in El Paso. Mills, charging Hart with the offense of false arrest and illegal confinement during the Civil War, had sued Hart in the district court and had been awarded $50,000 in damages. Hart had appealed the verdict to the Military Court. Hamilton, writing for the Court, denied the appeal on the technicality that it had not been made within the prescribed time limit of two years. Some historians have found it difficult to conclude that Hamilton was entirely impartial in this decision. At the time it was rendered, in October, 1868, Mills was courting Mary Hamilton, daughter of the Justice, and within five months would become Hamilton's son-in-law. Also, critics point out that Hamilton had demonstrated his unfriendliness to Hart when as Provisional Governor he had refused to approve the application of Hart for presidential amnesty on the ground that the El Pasoan had been a cotton speculator during the Civil War. Granting the possibility of bad feeling between the two men, nevertheless Hamilton seemed to have been on sound legal ground in deciding against Hart. When Hart later managed to bring his appeal before the Court again, after Hamilton was no longer a member, he was again denied relief.

While still a member of the Military Court, Hamilton played an important role in the Reconstruction Convention of 1868-1869, assembled to draft a new State constitution. This new instrument was to replace the more liberal constitution adopted in 1866; it was to implement more thoroughgoing Reconstruction. Plans to hold the convention and to elect delegates to it were soon under way.

General Charles Griffin, commanding the Military District of Texas, was charged before the removal of Governor J. W. Throckmorton with preparing a new list of voters. General Phil Sheridan had regarded Throckmorton as an impediment to Reconstruction. After the appointment of E. M. Pease as Provisional Governor, General Griffin took a further step. Since registration was slow, on September 2, 1867, he ordered the registrars to extend the registration period from the 23rd to the 28th of that month.[6] Meanwhile, General Sheridan had decided that the "Iron-clad" oath should be more strictly administered, a decision that discouraged many Conservative Democrats from applying for registration. The number of potential voters who were thus denied registration cannot be definitely determined, but the estimates vary from 7,500 to 10,000.[7]

As an essential step in changing the fundamental law of the State, on December 18, 1867, General Winfield S. Hancock, temporarily in command in Texas, ordered an

6. Charles William Ramsdell, *Reconstruction in Texas* (Columbia University Studies in History, Economics and Public Law, New York, 1910), Vol. XXXVI, No. I, p. 193.

7. *Ibid.*, p. 164, footnote 2; William A. Russ, Jr., "Radical Disfranchisement in Texas," *Southwestern Historical Quarterly*, XXXVIII, pp. 40-52.

election to be held in each county. It was called for February 10-14, 1868 to determine if a constitutional convention should be held, and to elect delegates to it.[8] General Hancock's proclamation stated that if more than fifty per cent of the registered voters participated in the election, the convention would be authorized. Conservative Democrats, though eager for the restoration of local government, feared that such a constitutional convention might enfranchise a large number of Negroes. Proceeding to hold a convention of their own in Houston, the Conservatives agreed to take part in the election, but to vote against calling a constitutional convention. At the same time they agreed to support those delegates who, if the question arose, would oppose Negro suffrage.[9] The Conservatives provided the majority of voters required to authorize the convention—a convention, however, that they could not control.

The convention duly approved by these maneuvers assembled in Austin on June 1, 1868. The ninety delegates who attended were divided into three groups: Conservatives, Moderate Republicans, and Radical Republicans. Some prominent leaders—such as Throckmorton, O. M. Roberts, Hardin R. Runnels, and John Ireland—were not among those participating. Not more than seven or eight delegates could be considered carpetbaggers; and not one of these was in fact influential. Several of the Radicals had served in the Confederate Army, and might be classified as scalawags. In spite of some opinion to the contrary, this was not a carpetbag convention, since its outstanding leaders—A. J. Hamilton, Edmund J. Davis, Morgan C. Hamilton, and James P. Newcomb—had long been identified with Texas. Lemuel Dale Evans, former Know-Nothing Congressman from the Eastern District of Texas, and James Armstrong, from Jasper County, were the leaders of the Conservatives. A. J. Hamilton, sup-

8. Ramsdell, *Reconstruction in Texas*, p. 195.
9. Ernest William Winkler (ed.), *Platforms of Political Parties in Texas* (Bulletin of the University of Texas, 1916, No. 53), pp. 104-106; Ramsdell, *Reconstruction in Texas*, p. 195.

ported by Justices Colbert Coldwell and Livingston Lindsay, associates on the Military Supreme Court, was leader of the Moderate Republicans. E. J. Davis, Morgan C. Hamilton, (brother of A. J.), James P. Newcomb, A. J. Evans, and Edward Degener were prominent Radicals.[10] Of the nine Negro delegates, G. T. Ruby and Ralph Long were the most prominent. The Negro delegates for the most part deported themselves well. They introduced sensible resolutions, voted as individuals and not as a group, and were better behaved than some of the white delegates.[11]

The convention chose sixteen regular committees. The recognized leaders of the different groups became chairmen of these standing committees. A. J. Hamilton was named to head the Judiciary Committee, and his brother Morgan C. served as chairman of the Committee on General Provisions.[12]

E. M. Pease, being only Provisional Governor, realized that he had no authority to make recommendations to the convention: nevertheless, he decided to send in a list of suggestions that he hoped would be helpful.[13] From the beginning, the deliberations of the convention were disturbed by the issue of *ab initio*. As interpreted by the Radical delegates, *ab initio* meant that the Secessionists had knowingly committed treasonable acts in voting for secession and in waging war against the United States. To accept this interpretation was in the view of the Radicals proof of being a true Republican. This doctrine of *ab initio* had embittered many delegates in the Convention of 1866 and it now threatened to disrupt the work of the present convention.

During the controversy over *ab initio* and other issues, A. J. Hamilton used his considerable influence in behalf of moder-

10. *Journal of the Reconstruction Convention Which Met at Austin, Texas, June 1, A.D., 1868* (Tracy, Siemering & Co., Printers, Austin, 1870), 1st Sess., 3-10, 20-25, 46. (Hereinafter cited as *Journal,* 1st Sess. or 2nd Sess.)

11. Harold Budd, "The Negro in Politics in Texas, 1868-1898" (M.A. thesis, University of Texas, Austin, 1925), pp. 23-24.

12. *Journal,* 1st Sess., pp. 3-10, 20-25, 46.

13. *Ibid.,* 1st Sess., pp. 12-17; *State Gazette,* March 11, June 5, 1868.

ation.[14] By this time, he had receded greatly from his earlier radical position. Several factors—the loss of his son John by premature death; the influence of sensible men like E. M. Pease, James H. Bell, and Thomas H. Duval; and his own basically sound judgment, when he permitted it to function— all these factors made for a more thoughtful and milder course than he had followed before.[15] On June 17, 1868, shortly after the convention met for the first time, he made what Editor A. H. Longley of the Austin *Republican* asserted was "an eloquent and unanswerable" reply to the extremists. He spoke in the same vein on several other occasions, notably on December 31, 1868, when he delivered a speech that the same newspaper described as "unsurpassed."[16]

Meanwhile, the Republicans in the convention were having difficulties. To deal with their intraparty differences, they held a special convention of their own in Austin, August 12-14, 1868. In this meeting, they became embroiled over *ab initio*. In fact, the Radicals, including E. J. Davis, withdrew and held their own rump convention.[17]

While all of this was taking place, the constitutional convention itself wrestled with difficult issues, such as the division of the State, lawlessness, and disfranchisement. Hamilton participated actively in all of the discussions about these issues. Even before the convention had assembled, the press of the State had raised the question of Texas dividing itself into several smaller states. The Resolution of Annexation,[18] enacted twenty-three years before, had authorized Texas to take this action if it decided to do so.

Governor Pease had proposed that instead of such division, the State should sell off much of the vast expanse of its western area—a move that would build up the School Fund,

14. Austin *Republican*, June 15, 17, 1868; *Journal*, 1st Sess., pp. 65-73.

15. A. J. Hamilton to E. M. Pease, October 28, 1867, in Graham-Pease Collection, Archives, Austin Public Library.

16. Austin *Republican, June* 15, 17, 1868, *Journal*, 1st Sess., pp. 65-73.

17. Winkler, *Platforms of Political Parties in Texas.* p. 115.

18. *Flake's Bulletin,* February 29, 1868.

subsidize railroad construction, and keep down State taxes.[19] W. W. Mills, delegate from El Paso County, proposed to alienate this county by combining it with Doña Ana County, New Mexico, to form the Territory of Montezuma. Presumably, this combination would become a political bailiwick for the sponsor of the plan.[20]

The possibility of dividing the State seemed to quicken the political ambitions of several other men who stood to profit from this course of action. E. J. Davis, for example, was one of the most persistent proponents of division. He apparently felt that at least part of Texas would fall under the control of the Republicans, with himself as their leader. His interest in division was prompted in no small degree by his belief that A. J. Hamilton, increasingly troublesome to the Radicals, might block Davis's political advancement if the State remained intact. With such a motivation, Davis and some of his supporters actually drafted a "Constitution for the State of West Texas."[21] As for A. J. Hamilton: he was opposed to division, though in seeking an acceptable compromise—or to confuse the matter—he offered his own plan for division.[22] Since his proposal proved unacceptable, Hamilton renewed his opposition to the several plans to divide the State. As a result, all of these plans failed, largely because of Hamilton's stand against them. Unfortunately, the convention spent many hours and much energy debating this issue; as a result, it moved at a snail's pace in writing the new constitution.[23]

The convention also discussed for days on end such matters as the persecution of freedmen and Unionists, and the extent

19. *Ibid.,* May 20, July 8, 1868; Governor's Message to the Convention, in *Journal,* 1st Sess., pp. 12-17.

20. *Ibid.,* 1st Sess., pp. 135, 758-761; *Flake's Bulletin,* July 8, 1868.

21. *Ibid.,* June 13, 16, 24, 27, 1868; Austin *Republican,* January 5, 6, 19, 1869; Ramsdell, *Reconstruction in Texas,* pp. 212-213; E. J. Davis to James P. Newcomb, May 2, 1875, in James P. Newcomb Collection, Archives, University of Texas Library.

22. Ramsdell, *Reconstruction in Texas,* p. 215.

23. Austin *Republican,* January 6, 1869; *Journal,* 1st Sess., pp. 12-17, 135, 144-148, 338, 391, 757-761; *Ibid.,* 2nd Sess., *passim;* Ramsdell, *Reconstruction in Texas,* p. 213.

of disorder and lawlessness in the State. These were indeed serious problems.[24] In his report of December 4, 1868, to the Adjutant General of the Army, General J. J. Reynolds emphasized the extent of lawlessness in East Texas, when he declared that "The civil law east of the Trinity River is almost a dead letter."[25] Even members of the constitutional convention were not immune from attacks. One of the white delegates, George W. Smith, and two or three Negroes, were taken from the jail in Jefferson, Marion County, by a mob and lynched.[26] Such acts of violence aggravated the tension and excitement prevalent in Texas. It was frequently asserted, with much justification, that crime was widespread west of the Brazos River and rampant east of it. In appraising conditions at the time, *Flake's Bulletin* took an objective view by arguing that the problem of crime was not so bad as unfriendly observers like General Sheridan and General Reynolds charged, but that it was possibly worse than most Texans would care to admit.[27]

A number of delegates at the convention felt that their sole duty was to draft a constitution that would meet the approval of the people of Texas and the Congress of the United States. Consequently, these delegates objected to the distractions and delays resulting from the discussions concerning lawlessness, the division of the State, and various extraneous or minor matters, such as the creation of new counties, railroad problems, the condition of the School Fund, and others.[28] Since A. J. Hamilton brought a number of these issues before the

24. A. H. Lattimer to E. M. Pease, January 8, 1867; M. C. Hamilton to E. M. Pease, November 9, 1866—both in Graham-Pease Collection, Archives, Austin Public Library; Colonel William S. Abert to A.G.O., June 9, August 3, 31, September 1, 2, 6, 1866, in A.G.O., Department of Texas, Book No. 3, National Archives.

25. *Flake's Bulletin,* December 16, 1868; Austin *Republican,* February 3, 1869; *Journal,* 2nd Sess., pp. 107-115.

26. Ramsdell, *Reconstruction in Texas,* pp. 230-231; B. W. Gray to Governor Pease, October 14, 1868, in Graham-Pease Collection, in Archives, Austin Public Library.

27. *Flake's Bulletin,* February 12, 19, 1868.

28. *Journal,* 1st Sess., pp. 66-71, 103, 107, 117, 121, 142, 464-470, 499, 758-761; *ibid.,* pp. 10, 12, 166, 170, to list a few problems considered.

convention, he must bear some responsibility for the delays in completing the draft of the constitution. He sponsored, and spent considerable time in working for, the international railroad scheme, the validation of Sam Houston's claim to 1,280 acres of land, and a proposal that the convention authorize the purchase of 3,500 copies of George W. Paschal's *Digest of the Laws of Texas*.[29]

As the convention labored on, by the end of June, 1868, *Flake's Bulletin* was thoroughly disillusioned as to the character and intelligence of many of the delegates. On one occasion, it remarked " . . . the less a man knows the wider he opens his mouth, and it is as impossible for a fool to keep his jaws shut as for a sick oyster to keep his shell closed." The Bulletin was especially critical of the preachers in the convention. In referring to the interminable sermons that the fourteen minister—delegates delivered, the newspaper wondered if they might not defeat the effort to draft a constitution.[30]

At the same time, *Flake's Bulletin* gave A. J. Hamilton the highest rating. Following his speech opposing the efforts of the Radical delegates to disfranchise the Conservatives, it declared: "Governor Hamilton is by far the greatest man in the Convention, and by this speech has exhibited to his colleagues, his opponents and to the world, that he has a heart that excels in generous impulses, and that he possesses oratorical powers that tower as the huge oak above the sapling, beyond any member in that body."[31]

In spite of the distractions, the convention delegates slowly proceeded with the main task before them. The various committees met fairly regularly, worked on their assignments, and made their reports. The judicial Committee under the chairmanship of A. J. Hamilton recommended in its report filed

29. *Ibid.*, 1st Sess. pp. 31, 190-193, 435, 510, 694, 709, 777, 827; James P. Hart, "George W. Paschal," *Texas Law Review*, XXVIII, pp. 23-42.
30. *Flake's Bulletin*, July 22, August 19, 1868.
31. *Ibid.*, December 6, 1868; January 16, 1869; Austin *Republican*, June 19, December 31, 1868; January 2, 1869.

July 22, 1868, that the judicial system of Texas should be organized as follows:

I. A Supreme Court of five justices would serve as the tribunal of last resort. Its members would be appointed by the Governor, with the advice of the Senate. Justices would be chosen for terms of fifteen years, with their terms staggered in such a way that one justice would retire every three years. The justice next in line for retirement would serve as Chief Justice of the Supreme Court. Salaries of the justices were to be $4,500 per annum. The Court would exercise appellate jurisdiction in civil cases; it was to intervene in criminal cases only if one or more of the justices decided that there had been error in the proceedings of one of the district courts. The Supreme Court could issue the writ of habeas corpus and could exercise other powers to enforce its decisions.

II. The district judges were to be appointed by the Governor, with the advice and consent of the Senate, for eight years. Each judge's salary was set at $3,500 per annum. This salary, though small by present-day standards, appears considerably larger when compared to the $2,500 that a Federal district judge received at that time. The State district judges were to appoint the sheriffs for the counties. The jurisdiction granted the district judges was very wide.

III. Justices of the peace were to be elective, the only elective officials in the judicial system. They were to exercise jurisdiction over minor cases. Also the justices of the peace, as a group in each county, were to perform the duties now discharged by the county commissioners' courts.

A month after Hamilton submitted the report of the Judicial Committee, the convention, acting as a committee of the whole, began considering it. By now Hamilton's influence had increased, and the report, with only minor changes, was adopted.[32]

In addition to giving attention to his own committee assignment, Hamilton showed considerable interest in the reports of other committees. He occasionally made worthwhile contributions to the proposals that thus came before the convention. For instance, as originally drafted by the Political and Legislative Committee, Section 6 of Article III of the new constitution was to read as follows: "All elections by the people shall be held at such time and places, in the several districts,

32. *Journal*, 1st Sess., pp. 25, 111, pp. 465-470, 818; *Flake's Bulletin*, August 1, 1868.

counties, cities or towns, as are now or may hereafter be designated by law." The section was adopted provisionally in this form. But later, after Hamilton had given the wording of Section 6 careful thought, he moved for its reconsideration. He then offered the following substitute version: "All elections for State, district, and county officers, except justices of the peace, shall be held at the county seats of the several counties, until otherwise provided by law, and the polls shall be opened for voting for four days from eight o'clock, A.M., until four o'clock, P.M., each day." The convention approved this substitute wording.

As will appear in the following chapter of this book, a technical question of considerable importance arose later with reference to the exact meaning of this provision in the constitution. It is to be noted that no semicolon appears in Hamilton's amended version of Section 6 of Article III. The semicolon does appear, however, after the word "law" in the text that the convention finally adopted when it approved the report of its Committee of Eleven on Revision. The Convention also eliminated the phrase, "except justices of the peace" as it had appeared in Hamilton's version. Whether Hamilton had inserted the semicolon in his original draft is of no importance, for he was present at the time the Committee on Revision submitted its wording of Section 6 of Article III; and he voted for the adoption of that section, with the semicolon placed after the word "law." The significance of this change, and of Hamilton's later role regarding it, will be discussed in the following chapter when attention is directed to the historic Semicolon Case.[33]

The convention continued its sessions to the end of August. Their funds now exhausted, and much of their energy and enthusiasm now spent, the delegates voted to adjourn to the first Monday in December.[34] The recess may have afforded them some rest, but it did not reduce their problems. When the delegates reassembled, they were obliged to decide a most

33. *Journal,* 1st Sess., pp. 561-567, 856-857; *ibid.,* 2nd Sess., pp. 225-226, 255-256, 394.　　　　　　　　　　　　　34. *Ibid.,* 1st Sess., p. 853.

serious issue: the constitutional requirements for voting, an issue which inferentially involved the question of disfranchisement. This issue had already caused much dissension; it had almost wrecked the convention during the last weeks of the summer meetings.[35]

The background of the controversy had begun two years before in the preparation for the Constitutional Convention of 1866. Hamilton, then acting as Provisional Governor, had attempted to prevent voters who required presidential amnesty from serving as delegates or voting in the election for delegates. After his break with President Johnson, Hamilton had gone to the extreme of endorsing the Congressional Plan of Reconstruction, which enfranchised the Negroes while disqualifying many of the outstanding Texas leaders as voters for delegates to the Reconstruction Convention.[36]

Concerning disfranchisement, various proposals were submitted to deny the ballot to all who had voted for secession; to editors and preachers who had advocated secession;[37] to Partisan Rangers who had persecuted Unionists; to those citizens who had fled from Texas after the collapse of the Confederacy; and to all persons who had been ruled ineligible to register and vote on the issue of assembling the present convention.[38]

As the Radical Republicans progressively hardened their attitude on disfranchisement, Hamilton, as leader of the Moderate Republicans, increasingly disagreed with their policies. He had come to feel that the Radical approach was both unwise and unjust. He believed that to disfranchise a

35. *Ibid.*, 2nd Sess., pp. 44-129, 287-288.
36. "Proclamations to the People of Texas," July 24 and September 11, 1865. Proclamation concerning election of delegates to Constitutional Convention of 1866—all in Executive Record Book No. 281, pp. 26, 192-194, 55-71, 124-128, Archives Division, Texas State Library; A. J. Hamilton, *An Address on "Suffrage and Reconstruction," the Duty of the People, the President, and Congress: Delivered at the Invitation of the Impartial-Suffrage League, at Tremont Temple in Boston, December 3, 1866* (Boston, Impartial-Suffrage League, Boston 1866), Archives, Austin Public Library.
37. Judge T. H. Duval to E. M. Pease, October 18, 1866, in Graham-Pease Collection, Archives, Austin Public Library; *Journal,* 2nd Sess., pp. 388, 464-467.
38. *Journal,* 1st Sess., pp. 12-17, 123, 125.

most intelligent group of citizens, while enfranchising the most ignorant and least prepared, would prevent the re-establishment of a republican form of government.[39] Governor Pease, along with other men of moderation, aligned them-selves with Hamilton. As a result, the Radicals were de-feated on perhaps the most crucial issue before the convention.

Having succeeded in blocking an unwise policy, Hamilton was now prepared to take affirmative action. On February 3, 1869, he introduced the following proposal: "Male citizens twenty-one years of age, resident of Texas at the time of the adoption of this Constitution, or who later live in the State one year, and in the county sixty days preceding election, unless disqualified by the Constitution of the United States, shall have the right to vote." A real struggle ensued. The Radicals resorted to various parliamentary moves to defeat the proposal. In the end, however, it was adopted—a victory that reflected much credit on Hamilton and on the majority of his fellow members.[40] Hamilton's service in restoring sanity and fairness to the voting process in Texas won him much gratitude and praise. Not only such leaders as O. M. Roberts, William G. Webb, and John H. Reagan, but also ordinary citizens throughout the State expressed admiration for him.[41]

Almost from the day the convention reassembled in De-cember, 1868, its meetings were marked by disturbances bordering on violence. One delegate was expelled,[42] a number were arrested, and finally the president of the convention, E. J. Davis, became so enraged at the disorders that he almost went berserk. On his own motion, he adjourned the con-vention—and, what was even worse, he refused to return to its sessions to restore order or to bring about an orderly ad-

39. Austin *Republican,* February 24, 1869.

40. *Journal,* 2nd Sess., pp. 387, 412, 415, 413, 483, 486, 518-520

41. Dudley G. Wooten (ed.), *A Comprehensive History of Texas, 1689-1897* (2 vols., W. G. Scarff, Dallas, 1898), II, p. 176; Houston *Telegraph,* September 25, 1869; Ben Hamill Procter, *Not Without Honor: A Biography of John H. Reagan* (University of Texas Press, Austin, 1962), p. 188.

42. *Journal,* 2nd Sess., pp. 44-129, p. 325; Austin *Republican,* January 25, 27, 1869.

122]   ANDREW JACKSON HAMILTON

journment.[43] Two of his supporters—George T. Ruby, one of the Negro delegates, and James P. Newcomb—resigned rather, as they said, than to continue associating with such a group. Their real motive, however, was to oppose the constitution nearing completion, even to block its approval, for they disagreed with a number of its basic provisions.[44]

In spite of the disorders, the convention was able to complete its work and set a date—the first Monday in July, 1869—for submitting the draft of the proposed constitution to the people of Texas for their approval. The same day was designated also for holding general elections—local, State, and congressional.[45] Since E. J. Davis did not return to the convention, M. L. Armstrong was chosen president pro tempore and served during its closing sessions. On February 8, the convention was declared adjourned.[46]

The *Journal* of the convention shows that it actually ended its work on February 6.[47] A. J. Bennett, a delegate, later wrote James P. Newcomb an account of the closing days. He reported during these days, Hamilton, usually under the influence of whiskey, attempted to speak on all occasions. Bennett also mentioned the lack of a quorum on Saturday, February 6, and explained that the group had adjourned to Monday, February 8, the final adjournment date.[48] According to reports then current, Bennett himself was arrested, and certain convention records were recovered from him.[49]

The Reconstruction Convention thus expired—none too nobly, but with some solid accomplishments. In spite of the confusion that marked its meetings, the 1868-69 Convention made fundamental political decisions with restraint and produced an acceptable and workable constitution for the State.

43. *Journal,* 2nd Sess., pp. 44-129, 287, 301, and pages for rest of the session; Austin *Republican,* February 2, 10, 1869.
44. Ibid., February 10, 17, 1869.   45. *Journal,* 2nd Sess., pp. 506-510
46. *Ibid.,* 2nd Sess., pp. 265-278, 394; Austin *Republican,* February 10, 1869.
47. *Journal,* 2nd Sess., p. 529.
48. A. J. Bennett to James P. Newcomb, February 8, 1869, in James P. Newcomb Collection, Archives, University of Texas.
49. Austin *Republican,* February 10, 1869.

CHAPTER IX

The End of Reconstruction

THE SUCCESS in drafting the Constitution of 1869 was an important advance in restoring normal relations between Texas and the National Government. This step had been taken in the course of long and bitter debate over such questions as disfranchisement and the subdivision of the State. The hostility of the Radicals in the convention that drafted the new constitution caused A. J. Hamilton and his friends and allies to prepare an appeal to Congress for acceptance of the new fundamental law for the State.

This appeal was in the form of a "Memorial to Congress," and it was dated March 16, 1869.[1] Hamilton contributed most of the content, it appears. The document sought to explain Hamilton's action in calling the Constitutional Convention of 1866 while he was Provisional Governor, and to explain the failure of the convention to carry out his suggestions. This fact implies that Hamilton was chiefly responsible for writing the appeal. By calling attention to the obstructive tactics of E. J. Davis and his supporters, the burden of the appeal indicated that Hamilton hoped to be accepted by the national leaders of the Republican Party as the head of the party in Texas.[2]

To press his appeal, Hamilton had left Austin for Washington in February, 1869. Within a few days, he in effect launched his campaign for Governor. On February 15, stopping off in Brenham, approximately eighty miles east of Austin, he delivered a significant speech to a mixed crowd of whites and Negroes. In the course of his remarks, he tried to clarify his actions in the constitutional convention, especially those

1. Austin *Republican,* March 31, April 5, 1869.
2. *Ibid.,* March 31, 1869.

relating to the question of disfranchisement. In doing so, he
made a direct appeal to the Negroes for their endorsement and
support by calling attention to the fact that he had been the
first official in Texas to work for their enfranchisement. At
the same time, he pointed out to them the injustice of giving
them the vote, while denying it to leading citizens of the State.
Continuing, he called on all his listeners, both white and black,
to be forgiving and to join in developing the rich treasures of
Texas for the good and glory of all. As for the new constitution, Hamilton conceded that it was not perfect, but insisted
that it was at least acceptable. He recommended it as the
best that could be written under the conditions confronting
the convention that had drafted it.[3]

Some four months before, early in November, 1868, General J. J. Reynolds had been transferred to Washington.
There he soon reestablished cordial relations with Grant, one
of his classmates at West Point. When Hamilton and his
group arrived in Washington, General Reynolds presented
them to Grant, now President-elect. On this occasion, Hamilton spoke highly of Reynolds and his administration in Texas.[4]
There was no complaint concerning the policies of General
E. R. S. Canby, who had succeeded Reynolds as commander
in Texas. But a feeling had developed among Republican
leaders that a wrong had been done Reynolds and that in
justice to him, he should be returned as head of the Federal
forces in Texas. In any event, Reynolds replaced Canby in
March, 1869. As later developments showed, the change
proved unfortunate for Hamilton.[5]

President Grant had now begun his first term. His first
nominations for political appointments in Texas were friends
of Hamilton's: John L. Haynes, to be Collector of Customs
at Galveston; H. C. Pedigo, Assessor of Internal Revenue at
Galveston; F. W. Sumner, Assessor of the Northern District

3. *Ibid.*, February 24, 1869.
4. *Ibid.*, November 6, 7, 13, 1868; April 8, 1869; Charles Williams Ramsdell,
Reconstruction in Texas (Columbia University Studies in History, Economics
and Public Law, New York, 1910), p. 228.
5. *State Gazette,* March 5, 1869; Ramsdell, *Reconstruction in Texas,* p. 266.

of Texas; James A. McKie, Postmaster at Galveston; A. H. Longley, editor of the Austin *Republican,* one of the revenue collectors.[6]

Hamilton himself, while in Washington, received support from the politically influential Washington *Chronicle.* For a time, it seemed that he had not only won congressional approval of the newly drafted Texas constitution but had also won the confidence of President Grant and other leaders of the Republican Party.[7] Nevertheless, Hamilton had enemies in Congress—loyal friends of former President Andrew Johnson—as shown by the attack that Senator Samuel J. Randall made on Hamilton in a public place. When Randall called Hamilton a "'damned scoundrel," a fight ensued. During the altercation, the Texan struck the Senator with his cane, knocking him down.[8] Later, Hamilton encountered more trouble, when a group headed by E. J. Davis came to Washington from Texas. The Davis group made the trip to oppose the new Texas constitution and Hamilton's efforts to extend his political power in the State. Meanwhile, General Reynolds' return to military control in Texas signaled a move toward Radicalism.[9] The Republican Party of the State was soon rent apart, never again to be completely united during the lives of the early leaders.[10]

The next development in Hamilton's career followed in the spring. When rumors began to circulate in Texas that the general election on the new constitution would be delayed, Hamilton dispatched a telegram from Washington to quell the reports. The constitutional convention had set the first Monday in July, 1869, as the date for the election, which would entail a vote on the adoption of the proposed

6.   Austin *Republican,* April 9, 1869.

7.   *Ibid.,* April 5, 1869.

8.   *Flake's Bulletin,* May 27, 1868.

9.   *Ibid.,* July 14, August 7, 14, 18, October 6, 1869; Austin *Republican,* June 24, October 20, 1869; Ernest William Winkler (ed.), *Platforms of Political Parties in Texas* (Bulletin of the University of Texas, 1916, No. 53), p. 107.

10.   James P. Newcomb Correspondence, 1869-1873, Archives, University of Texas Library.

constitution and the choice of officials, both State and local.[11] Hamilton's telegram assured the public that the election would be held on the day authorized. Unhappily for him, Hamilton proved to be in error; the election, it turned out, would not be held until late November.[12] In the meantime, on March 18, Hamilton announced his candidacy for Governor, using the newspapers of the State for this purpose. He did not trust his hopes to a nominating convention, preferring instead the democratic way of running in an open field.[13]

On June 7-8, 1869, a group of Radical Republicans held a nominating convention in Houston. James G. Tracy, editor and publisher of the Houston *Union,* and James P. Newcomb, editor of the San Antonio *Express,* organized the meeting, which was attended by approximately thirty delegates from sixteen counties. The assembly nominated E. J. Davis for Governor and James W. Flanagan for Lieutenant Governor. Although the leaders of this group had attempted to prevent the drafting of the new constitution, they now decided to recommend its approval in the forthcoming election.[14] The fact that even this small convention was held, and the further fact that Hamilton did not receive the endorsement of any convention for the governorship, militated against him in the North. Some of his supporters urged John L. Haynes, chairman of the Republican State Executive Committee, to call a convention for the purpose of nominating Hamilton and thus to offset the advantage that Davis had gained. But Hamilton opposed the move on the ground that a convention would result only in further bickering and a deeper division in the Republican Party.[15]

11. *Journal of the Reconstruction Convention Which Met at Austin, Texas, June 1, A.D., 1868* (Tracy, Siemering & Co., Printers, Austin, 1870), 2nd Sess., pp. 506-510.

12. *Tri-Weekly State Gazette,* April 21, July 21, 1869.

13. Austin *Republican,* March 24, April 1, May 22, 1869.

14. Winkler, *Platforms of Political Parties in Texas,* pp. 119-120; M. C. Hamilton to James P. Newcomb, May 6, 1869, in James P. Newcomb Collection, Archives, University of Texas Library.

15. Austin *Republican,* April 1, May 22, 1869.

Rumors began to circulate hinting at a sort of Republican solidarity. According to one report, E. J. Davis was willing to accept second place on a ticket headed by Hamilton. This idea was closely associated with another: that Hamilton in reality wanted to become a United States Senator. Thus, if Hamilton and Davis ran as a team and won, Hamilton by resigning could make it possible for Davis to succeed to his office. The State Legislature, controlled by Davis and Hamilton, would then name the latter to the position in Washington. Regardless of whether there was any basis for this rumor, it may have been a factor in Hamilton's defeat.[16]

Another rumor that may have hurt Hamilton's chances was to the effect that he had sold out to the Conservative Democrats. The main assumption of this hypothesis was that the Democrats would elect majorities in both houses of the Legislature and that Hamilton would then work with them. No doubt, many of the Democrats who intended to vote for Hamilton insisted also on the election of a Conservative Democratic Legislature.[17] A number of Democratic leaders, including John H. Reagan and Ashbel Smith, agreed to support Hamilton and at the same time to work for Democratic control of the Legislature.[18] Some of the Democratic leaders, notably Reagan, were willing to vote for approval of the new constitution. Reagan endorsed it in a speech delivered in Palestine, Texas, on September 24. In the speech he also pledged his support to Hamilton as candidate for Governor.[19]

In addition, a number of prominent Democratic editors agreed to support Hamilton. Among them were Robert

16. *Flake's Bulletin,* March 10, 20, 1869; E. J. Davis to James P. Newcomb, June 24, 1869; G. C. Rives, to James P. Newcomb, June 18, 1869—both in James P. Newcomb Collection, Archives, University of Texas Library.

17. Winkler, *Platforms of Political Parties in Texas,* pp. 108-109; *State Gazette,* April 7, 12, 19, 26, June 23, 25, 30, 1869.

18. Ashbel Smith to John Hancock and W. M. Walton, February 22, 1869; John H. Reagan to Ashbel Smith, February 23, 1869—all in Ashbel Smith Papers (1823-1886), Archives, University of Texas Library; John H. Reagan, March 9, 1869, to W. G. Webb, Editor, Houston *Telegraph,* in John H. Reagan Papers, 1847-1905, Archives, University of Texas Library.

19. *Ibid.; Flake's Bulletin,* October 9, 1869.

Josselyn of the *State Gazette* and Willard Richardson of the Galveston *News*. While endorsing Hamilton, they intended also to work for the control of the Legislature by their party. They favored foregoing a State Democratic convention in order to achieve their objectives more effectively. As for the Republican newspapers, the only ones to give Hamilton enthusiastic support were the Austin *Republican* and *Flake's Bulletin*. When on one occasion Flake was accused of drifting, he replied: "To the unstable mariner tossed about by the waves of the sea, the everlasting hills appear to be dancing a jig."[20]

Other editors were much less enthusiastic over Hamilton's candidacy. Only one of the nineteen weekly newspapers east of the Trinity gave him active support. The Houston *Union* and San Antonio *Express* came out strongly in support of Davis.[22] In fact, the editors of these two newspapers had organized the June convention that nominated him. A few unreconciled, unreconstructed editors refused to accept either Hamilton or Davis. These irreconcilables included R. W. Loughery (*Texas Republican* and Jefferson *Times*), Victor W. Thompson (*States' Rights Democrat*), and Hamilton Stuart (Galveston *Civilian*). During September 29-30, they held an editors' convention in Brenham and nominated Hamilton Stuart for Governor. It was soon rumored that Davis had promised Stuart some of the printing patronage of the State—a rumor that subsequently proved true.[23]

By the spring of 1869, Davis had emerged as spokesman of the Radicals. Not long after General Reynolds had returned to the Texas command, he began in earnest to appoint Radicals to civilian offices under him.[24] In a number of

20. *State Gazette*, April 7, 19, May 26, 1869; Winkler, *Platforms of Political Parties in Texas*, p. 108; Austin *Republican*, March-November, 1869; *Flake's Bulletin*, May 1, and March-November, 1869.

21. *Flake's Bulletin*, May 22, 1869.

22. *Ibid.*, through campaign, June-November, 1869.

23. Winkler, *Platforms of Political Parties in Texas*, p. 122; E. J. Davis to James P. Newcomb, James P. Newcomb Collection, Archives, University of Texas Library, *Tri-Weekly State Gazette*, October 8, 1869.

24. *Ibid.*, September 18, 29, October 6, 1869.

instances, he removed friends of Hamilton from office to make way for supporters of Davis.[25] Reynolds in October gave further evidence of his partiality in a letter to President Grant. The letter urged support for Davis as leader of the true Republican Party in Texas.[26] When the contents of this letter became known, Provisional Governor Pease was offended to the point of resigning rather than be a party, as it were, to the betrayal of Hamilton.[27]

It is clear that Reynolds had been promised a worthwhile reward for his support in the event that Davis should become Governor. After being elected Governor, Davis paid his debt by inducing the Legislature to name Reynolds United States Senator.[28] Davis hoped thus to displace A. J. Hamilton's brother, Morgan C. Hamilton. The latter had been elected for the term ending March 4, 1871, and for the following term, ending March 4, 1877.[29] Davis was able to convince a sufficient number of his henchmen in the Legislature that Morgan Hamilton had not been legally elected to the full term, or else had forfeited it by failure to perform his duties properly. Yet, when a Committee of the United States Senate investigated the issue, the incumbent was able successfully to defend his right to the office. By recommending that Morgan Hamilton should retain his seat, the Committee defeated Davis' and Reynolds' ambitions.[30]

The general election in November, 1869, was marked by considerable apathy, especially among the white voters.[31] The

25. *Flake's Bulletin,* October 6, 1868; Austin *Republican,* October 6, 1869.
26. *Ibid.*
27. Provisional Governor E. M. Pease to General J. J. Reynolds, September 30, 1869, in Graham-Pease Collection, Archives, Austin, Texas, Public Library.
28. *Journal of the Senate, Twelfth Legislature of Texas* (J. G. Tracy, State Printer, Austin, 1871), pp. 67-68; Austin *Republican,* January 3, 1870.
29. *Journal of the Senate of the State of Texas, Provisional Session of 1870,* and *Journal of the House of Representatives of the State of Texas* (bound in one volume, Tracy, Siemering & Co., Austin, 1870), pp. 61-62.
30. Houston *Telegraph,* January 20, February 10, July 22, October 13, 1871; Walter Prescott Webb and H. Bailey Carroll (eds.), *The Handbook of Texas* (2 vols., Texas State Historical Association, Austin, 1952), II, p. 466; *Congressional Globe,* 42 Cong., 1st Sess., Pt. I, pp. 168, 169.
31. Austin *Republican,* December 22, 1869; *Flake's Bulletin,* December 11, 1869; *Tri-Weekly State Gazette,* December 8, 1869.

election had been postponed to the last days of the month, a time of miserable weather throughout most of the State.[32] Numerous irregularities occurred during the balloting, and there was much violence in several places. The votes of two counties, Milam and Navarro, were thrown out. The vote was close: General Reynolds, who had the last word, decided that 39,901 votes had been cast for Davis and 39,002 for Hamilton.[33] Davis' victory resulted to a great extent from the apathy of the white voters and the firm support of well-organized Negro groups. It is probable that Hamilton went to his grave convinced that Reynolds had unfairly counted him out. Certainly, many of his friends felt that way.

Shortly after announcing victory for Davis, General Reynolds filled the void created by Pease's resignation two months before the election. In December, Reynolds appointed Davis and all other elected officials to act in a provisional capacity until their regular terms began. Reynolds also convened the Legislature on February 8, 1870.[34] It approved the Thirteenth, Fourteenth and Fifteenth amendments to the National Constitution—a signal for Congress to accept the Texas Constitution of 1869. The Legislature also elected Morgan C. Hamilton and James W. Flanagan to the Senate in Washington, which certified them as members. After the Legislature had taken these steps, Reynolds proclaimed the end of military control in Texas and turned over all civil authority to Governor Davis and the other elected officials. The Provisional Legislature which had convened on February 8, now adjourned sixteen days later, February 24, 1870.[35]

Meanwhile, President Grant proclaimed that Texas had been restored to the Union. Immediately thereafter, Governor Davis issued a proclamation convening the Twelfth Legisla-

32. *Ibid.*, December 3, 1869.

33. *Flake's Bulletin,* December 25, 1869; Ramsdell, *Reconstruction in Texas,* 283-296.

34. *Journal of Senate and Journal of the House of Representatives,* Provisional Legislature (bound in one volume), *op. cit.,* pp. 14, 26, 55, 36, 50, 51.

35. *Ibid.,* pp. 29, 30, 42, 46.

ture on April 26, 1870.[36] His message contained a series of proposals which, enacted into law, would create a political despotism.[37] The most offensive of the proposals, especially after they had been put into operation, were for acts creating a State Militia and a State Police. Governor Davis believed that armed authority must be available under his control, strong enough to break up, or destroy, or drive out of the State organized bands of outlaws. With a well-organized militia subject to the Governor's call, and an effective police force always at his command, Davis knew that he could act quickly and effectively as he might decide.

In addition, the Radical Governor sought the power to suspend the civil courts and to institute martial law as a means of crushing resistance. He insisted that the county in which lawless groups operated should be obliged to pay all expenses entailed in restoring law and order. This require-ment, he declared, would have a sobering effect on both the lawless bands and the local law-enforcing agencies. It soon became clear, however, that the enforcement of this feature of the Militia Act by the use of Negroes as members of the Militia would antagonize and estrange the white population of Texas more than any other feature of Reconstruction.[38]

Among the most reprehensible aspects of Davis' program were the strong-arm methods to which the Radical leaders in the Legislature resorted. Members of that body who re-fused to accede to the program were arrested and excluded from voting on it. By these arbitrary tactics—surely a travesty

36.   Proclamation of Governor E. J. Davis, April 12, 1870, *Journal of the House of Representatives,* Twelfth Legislature, 1st Sess., p. 3.

37.   Message of Governor Davis, April 29, 1870, *Ibid.,* 17-31; *State Gazette,* May 2, 1870, and throughout the spring and summer of 1870; Austin *Republican,* May 25, 1870, and following issues, reflecting increased bitterness; the same for other newspapers, except the subsidized Republican papers.

38.   Otis A. Singletary, "The Texas Militia during Reconstruction," *Southwest-ern Historical Quarterly,* LX, pp. 21-26; Walter Prescott Webb, *The Texas Rangers: A Century of Frontier Defense* (Houghton Miflin Company, Boston and New York, c. 1935), pp. 224-229; H. P. N. Gammel, *Laws of Texas,* (10 vols., Austin, 1898), VI, pp. 185-190, 193-195.

on the democratic process—Davis and his henchmen established autocratic control over the government and people of Texas.[39]

A. J. Hamilton followed these developments with growing concern. At last, thoroughly aroused—and encouraged by the editor of the Austin *Republican* and other friends—Hamilton announced that he would speak out. On Saturday evening, July 23, 1870, he appeared in the hall of the House of Representatives in Austin, which was open to such events. Here he courageously reviewed the various high-handed acts of Governor Davis and the Twelfth Legislature. In doing so, he delivered one of the most scorching philippics known in the history of Texas.

Although Hamilton realized that his defiance would provoke his critics, he declared that the situation was too grave to be ignored, regardless of the criticism and risk involved. Although he might be accused of "being activated by personal resentment and defeated ambition," he insisted that Governor Davis, while he operated ostensibly under the liberal State Constitution recently adopted and the Federal Constitution was in fact "a narrow-minded, bigoted, corrupt and blindly ambitious petty despot," backed up by a subservient Legislature. The Governor had not only increased the tax burden to oppressive proportions, with the danger that the people of the State would be saddled with an almost unbearable bonded indebtedness; he had also built up a despotism that threatened to destroy all the precious rights and liberties won over hundreds of years by the English-speaking peoples.

In his denunciation of the Davis regime, Hamilton took up each of the Governor's acts in turn and showed how it would affect adversely the economic and political wellbeing of the people. He modeled his speech somewhat on Mark Antony's oration over the dead body of Julius Caesar in Shakespeare's play. Hamilton scornfully repeated the expression, "But friends say Governor Davis is a good man, and will

39. Austin *Republican*, June 8, July 27, 1870.

not abuse his powers." Hamilton insisted that the very fact
that the Governor asked for the powers proved that he meant
to use them. Davis' tax measures, according to Hamilton,
involved the virtual confiscation of the wealth of the people—
a most deplorable outcome.

Yet this economic threat was nothing as compared to the
dangers to the freedom and security of the individual. Hamilton feared for the right of the private citizen to live his life
free of molestation by arbitrary authority such as the State
Militia and the State Police, subject entirely to the will of the
Governor. The speaker was especially shocked at the legislative act making all local peace officers—sheriffs, deputies,
constables, and urban police—subservient to the Governor.
He therefore urged all possible opposition by peaceable means
to these oppressive laws—opposition such as appeals to the
courts, petitions to the Legislature, and appeals to Congress.
As for the legislators immediately responsible for the laws,
Hamilton denounced them as ignorant men who had not
even read the Constitution of Texas or of the United States.
And he added for good measure that if they went down in
history as a "set of asses," he would not defend them.[40]

Shortly after Hamilton had delivered this defiant address,
he announced that he favored the repeal of some of the
congressional measures relating to Reconstruction. He explained his position succinctly as follows: "Civil and constitutional liberty is, with me, above party ties. . . . The time
for the repeal of disabilities and test oaths has arrived. Intelligence and virtue must be left free to combat ignorance and
cupidity, or the end of free government is near at hand."[41]

Hamilton's outspoken attack on Governor Davis embold-
ened others to take up the fight. Within a short time, J. W.
Throckmorton and other influential leaders of the Democratic
Party were aroused. They began maneuvering with Hamil-

40. A. J. Hamilton, *An Address* (printed at the office of the Austin *Republican*,
1870); *Daily State Journal,* July 20, 1870.

41. A. J. Hamilton to George W. Booker, August 10, 1870, in Austin *Republican,* August 24, 1870.

ton and his staunch friends like E. M. Pease to win control of the Legislature.[42] The Davis-dominated legislators, however, prolonged their terms of office for one year by a simple, though wholly unconstitutional, act. They postponed the ensuing election beyond the date set by law.[43]

Meanwhile, opposition to the Radicals was steadily building up. The reaction was evidenced by editorials in the *State Gazette*, then under the management of Victor W. Thompson, S. G. Sneed, and John D. Elliott. One editorial after another insisted on a return to "First Principles," the restoration of Texas under "the Constitution [of the United States] as it was." This position apparently did not recognize the Thirteenth, Fourteenth, and Fifteenth amendments as integral parts of the Constitution.[44]

Thompson of the *Gazette* at one point became enraged over a statement attributed to Senator Morgan C. Hamilton. He was quoted to the effect that unreconstructed Southerners in general, and Texans east of the Trinity River in particular, "were the most blood-thirsty set of cut-throats that God ever permitted on his footstool." Thompson countered by describing the Senator as an "ingrate traitor," whose "record of passion . . . would scarcely be blotted out by the tears of a heavenly host of weeping angels".[45]

The *State Gazettte* refused to support A. J. Hamilton, in spite of his then moderate position on Reconstruction. Its editors claimed that as a Unionist he had betrayed the people of Texas in their hour of need, and that during Reconstruction he had vilified the leading men of the State. "These things," the newspaper averred, "are matters of history, and

42. *Ibid.*, July 27, October 5, 19, December 21, 1870; *State Gazette*, July 25, 1870.

43. Houston *Telegraph*, April 25, May 17, 1871; James Pearson Newcomb, "Vindication of the Republican Administration of Texas" (paperbound clipping of letter sent by Newcomb, October 16, 1871, to editor of Chicago *Tribune*, and now in Eugene Campbell Barker Texas History Center, University of Texas Library), p. 2.

44. *Tri-Weekly State Gazette*, April 13, 20, July 4, 18, October 12, 14, 1870.

45. *Ibid.*, April 27, 29, 1870.

have caused the name of Hamilton to stink in the nostrils of all men who prefer the approval of their own consciences, to the reward of venality and corruption".[46]

In spite of opposition from irreconcilables like Thompson, Sneed, and Elliott, leaders of the Democratic Party faced the election with increased confidence. The Congressional Amnesty Act of 1870 had restored the franchise to many prominent Texans who had supported the Confederacy; it was clear that they would soon make their political influence felt.[47] In addition, many disillusioned Conservative Republicans like E. M. Pease and the Hamilton brothers joined with the Democrats in opposing the policies of E. J. Davis. With Pease acting as president of the gathering, a tax-payers' convention met in Austin in September, 1871. A. J. Hamilton served as one of its committee chairmen. The convention promptly drew up a series of resolutions denouncing the Davis administration.[48] After this independent meeting had adjourned, Governor Davis replied by a crude and irrational display of irritation. Accompanied by a large body of Negroes and Radicals, he marched around the legislative hall where the convention had just met, protesting its action. The resolutions passed by the convention were nevertheless given widespread publicity.

The resolutions came at a time of growing opposition to the excesses of the Davis regime. This opposition increased rapidly and effectively.[49] First, the Democrats won a decisive victory in the congressional election of October 1, 1871.[50] Then, the following year, they gained control of the lower house of the State Legislature and strengthened the conservative segment in the State Senate. It now became possible for the Democrats to determine policies by threatening to withhold appropriations. Using this strategy, the Democratic Conservatives were able to force the repeal of the objection-

46. *Ibid.,* September 5, 1870.   47. *United States Statutes,* XVI, pp. 614-630.
48. Houston *Telegraph,* August 5, September 27, 1871.
49. *Ibid.,* September 27, 28, 1871.
50. *Ibid.,* October 10, 1871; Ramsdell, *Reconstruction in Texas,* p. 310.

able acts of the previous Legislature, or at least to modify
the effects of such acts by denying Governor Davis the power
to use the State Militia, or to control future elections by alter-
ing the dates fixed by law.[51] There was considerable talk of
impeaching Davis, but the Governor averted this move. Real-
izing that he had been checkmated, he adjusted his policies to
the new realities that confronted him.[52]

The general election of 1873 was one of the most important
in the history of Texas. Although the Radical Republican
leaders made every affort to win, they—including Davis and
most of his legislative supporters—were roundly defeated.
But Governor Davis and his coterie were not willing to accept
the verdict at the polls. As poor losers, they attempted to
prove the election itself illegal. Specifically, they charged
that the law under which the election had been held was
unconstitutional. In the celebrated case of *Ex parte Rodríguez*
decided in the State Supreme Court (39 Tex. 706), the Radical counsel argued that the election law of March 31, 1873,
conflicted with Section 6 of Article III of the Constitution
of 1869, now governing.[53]

It will be recalled that Hamilton was the author of the
constitutional provision to which the Radicals now appealed.
The provision reads as follows: "All elections for State, district,
and county officers, shall be held at the county seats of the
several counties, until otherwise provided by law; and the
polls shall be opened four days, from eight o'clock A.M.
until four o'clock P.M. of each day.[54] On March 31, 1873,
the Legislature enacted an election law containing the following section: All the elections in the State shall be held
for one day only at each election, and the polls shall be

51. Seth Shepard McKay, *Seven Decades of the Texas Constitution of 1876*
(Lubbock, Pref. 1942) p. 42; Ramsdell, *Reconstruction in Texas*, pp. 313-314.

52. *Tri-Weekly State Gazette*, December 6, 9, 13, 1872.

53. McKay, *Seven Decades of the Texas Constitution of 1876*, pp. 43-44.

54. *Journal of the Reconstruction Convention, 1868-1869*, op. cit., 1st Sess.,
561, 856-857; *ibid.*, 2nd Sess., pp. 256, 394.

open on that day from 8 o'clock A.M. to 6 o'clock P.M." In accordance with this law, the general elections were held the first week in December.[55]

On December 16, 1873, Joseph Rodríguez inferentially challenged the legality of the election just held. He did so by applying to the State Supreme Court for a writ of habeas corpus on the ground that he was being held under arrest illegally. At the hearing, John Price, deputy sheriff of Harris County, admitted to the arrest and detention of Rodríguez on the basis of a warrant issued by a justice of the peace of Harris County. Rodríguez was charged with having voted illegally more than once in the general election in December, 1873.[56] At issue in the proceeding was the technical effect on the election law of 1873 of the semicolon in Section 6 of Article III of the constitution.

Did the authority of the Legislature to change the place of voting, as clearly shown in the first clause of Section 6, Article III, extend also to determining the time of voting? A. J. Hamilton, who had agreed to represent Rodríguez before the Court, argued that the State Constitution did not grant the Legislature power to fix the dates of elections. If this version was correct, Rodríguez had committed no offense, since the election in which he had voted irregularly was itself null and void.[57] In view of Hamilton's unhappy relations with the Radicals of the Republican Party, his role in this case appears strange indeed. Was it true, as A. W. Terrell wrote a friend, that the Republican leaders of all shades of opinion had closed ranks to face the threat of a revived, well-organized, and militant Democratic Party? Had the Republicans, in fact, "kissed all around the circle," as Terrell insisted?[58] Had

55. Gammel, *Laws of Texas,* VII, p. 472.
56. Ex Parte Rodríguez, *Texas Reports,* XXXIX, p. 706.
57. *Ibid.*
58. A. W. Terrell to O. M. Roberts, January 5, 1873, in O. M. Roberts' Letters, IV, MS. 8206, Archives, University of Texas Library; Boulds Baker to James P. Newcomb, September 26, 1874, in James P. Newcomb Collection, Archives, University of Texas Library.

Hamilton himself come to terms with the oppressive Radical organization which he had recently so boldly opposed?

The first move of counsel for the State of Texas, including A. W. Terrell, was to appeal to the Court for dismissal of the case. Justice McAdoo, speaking for the Court, denied the appeal, and ordered the lawyers on both sides to proceed with the trial.[59] The arguments of counsel for both plaintiff and defendant were shot through with bitter recriminations. For example, Terrell charged that Hamilton had deliberately trumped up the case for the purpose of denying to the Democratic Party the fruits of its decisive victory in the election. Hamilton replied caustically that he would accept no innuendos from those who had dragged the American flag in the mire and had tried to destroy the greatest nation on earth.[60] The feeling in the courtroom became so intense that lawyers for the State directed some of their invective at the members of the Court. The justices were accused of being motivated by personal interest in accepting the case for review—and possibly in the decision they would render. An amendment adopted in the election of 1873 had authorized the Governor-elect to appoint a new panel of justices to the Court.[61] By ruling that the election law of 1873 was unconstitutional, it was alleged, the judges could prevent this outcome and retain their positions.[62] At the end of the hearing, the majority of justices, whatever their motives, held that the election law indeed violated the Constitution of the State and thus was null and void.

The decision caused much criticism of the Court—in fact, the stigma of the decision plagued it for years to come. Rodríguez left the courtroom a free man, for he had committed no crime in voting irregularly in an illegal election.[63] Hamilton emerged from the case with a legal victory, but with his

59. Ex Parte Rodríguez, *Texas Reports*, XXXIX, p. 706.   60. *Ibid.*
61. Dudley G. Wooten (ed)., *A Comprehensive History of Texas, 1685-1897* (2 vols., W. G. Scarff, Dallas, 1898), II, p. 209.
62. Ex Parte Rodríguez, *Texas Reports*, XXXI, p. 706.
63. Wooten, *A Comprehensive History of Texas,* II, p. 201.

reputation tarnished by the general impression that he sacrificed principle for political expediency.[64]

As could have been expected, the decision of the Supreme Court —a decision aimed at voiding the election of 1873 and the Democratic victory won in it—by no means disposed of the basic issue. This issue was political, not legal, and it could not be settled by applying the technical rules of statutory construction. Thoroughly aroused by what they regarded as a political trick, the Democratic leaders refused to accept the Court's decree. Instead, they resolved to use all means possible to implement the will of the majority as expressed in the election.[65]

Sensing trouble from the embattled Democrats, legislative supporters of Governor Davis entrenched themselves in the assembly room of the Capitol, and at the same time Davis called on President Grant for support. At the height of the excitement, the Governor threatened to use the State Militia against his opponents—but fortunately several cooler heads among his followers dissuaded him from doing so.[66] Soon word came from the President, who "advised that it would 'be prudent as well as right' to accept the verdict of the voters," in the words of Historian Rupert N. Richardson.[67] Owing to this setback, together with the firm support that Richard Coke had received throughout the State in the gubernatorial race of 1873, Davis yielded to the popular will.

The vote was two to one in favor of the Democratic candidate for Governor: 85,549 for Coke to 42,633 for Davis. The

64. *Journal of the Reconstruction Convention, 1868-1869,* 2nd Sess., pp. 387, 412, 414, 485-486, 518-520.

65. James R. Norvell, "The Reconstruction Courts of Texas, 1867-1873," *Southwestern Historical Quarterly,* LXII, p. 153. Ex Parte Rodríguez, *Texas Reports,* XXXIX, p. 706; Ramsdell, *Reconstruction in Texas,* p. 317.

66. T. B. Wheeler, "Reminiscences of Reconstruction in Texas," *Quarterly of the Texas State Historical Association,* XI, pp. 56-65; Seth Shepard McKay, "The E. J. Davis Regime" (M.A. thesis, University of Texas, 1919), p. 152; William Curtiss Nunn, "Texas Under the Administration of E. J. Davis" (Ph. D. dissertation, University of Texas 1938), pp. 160-176.

67. Rupert N. Richardson, *Texas: The Lone Star State* (Prentiss-Hall Inc., New York, 1943), p. 284.

hold of the Radicals was thus broken at last. The Coke administration was installed, and Reconstruction for all practical purposes came to an end.[68] The Democrats dominated the election held two years later to choose delegates to the convention which wrote a new constitution for the State—the instrument that serves as the basic law to the present day.

Hamilton's appearance in the Semicolon Case was his last public act of consequence. At the end of his exciting career, he now welcomed the opportunity to retire to his farm a short distance east of the Capitol in Austin. Fortunately for him and his family, his brother Morgan in the late 1860's and early 1870's had distributed much of his wealth among his brothers and sister. A. J. Hamilton's share enabled him to improve the farm and build the kind of house he had long desired—a place beautiful and commodious, to which he gave the name "Fair Oaks."[69]

While working on the farm, Hamilton attempted to solve the personal problem that had plagued him most of his adult life. Writing to his daughter Mary and her husband, W. W. Mills, he declared that he was "full of hope and confidence and . . . equal to any reasonable emergency since I have swaped [sic] whiskey for ale, buttermilk, ice water & . . . " Later, he wrote again, saying that he had resolved not to drink a drop of liquor on that day or on any other throughout the year ahead.[70]

Excessive drinking, however, was not the only problem confronting Hamilton. Surprisingly, for a man of his size, strength,

68. Ramsdell, *Reconstruction in Texas*, pp. 313-317.

69. A. J. Hamilton to W.W. Mills, June 21, 1871; A. J. Hamilton to Mary Hamilton Mills, November 5, 1871—both in A. J. Hamilton Papers, Archives, University of Texas Library; Morgan C. Hamilton's will, made at San Diego, California, October 7, 1893; Probate Minutes, Book U, Travis County, Texas, p. 543.

70. A. J. Hamilton to Mary Hamilton Mills, January 1, 1872, A. J. Hamilton Papers, Archives, University of Texas Library; A. J. Hamilton to W. W. Mills, June 21, 1871, in *ibid*. S. M. Swenson to E. M. Pease, June 17, 1865; George W. Paschal to E. M. Pease, February 21, 1867—both in Graham-Pease Collection, Archives, Austin, Public Library.

and energy, he had contracted tuberculosis, the dread disease that often proved fatal in those days. To arrest the progress of the malady, Dr. Ferdinand Herff of San Antonio, well-known specialist in respiratory ailments, was called in for a series of treatments; but in spite of his efforts, the patient became progressively worse. Hamilton seemed not to be aware of the seriousness of his condition, or he was unwilling to admit to his plight. On April 10, 1875, he went downtown in Austin, where he met his old friend E. M. Pease, to whom he remarked that he felt confident of soon being able once again to attend to business.[71] But the next morning while at home, Hamilton was suddenly overcome with an attack of coughing—accompanied by a hemorrhage that promptly caused his death.[72] He was sixty years of age at the time.

Hamilton's life ended on a note of irony. With his retirement to Fair Oaks, it seemed that the former Unionist and Reconstruction Governor, after one of the most exacting careers in Texas history, had at last found tranquility. He could now, it appeared, live out his remaining time in contentment with his family and friends—free of controversy and economically secure.[73] To enjoy the rewarding months ahead, he needed only to survive. But death struck inexorably that April morning of 1875 on the farm near Austin, with no concern for the reward that Hamilton may well have deserved. The

71. Pat Ireland Nixon, *A History of the Texas Medical Association, 1853-1953* (University of Texas Press, Austin, 1953), pp. 14, 77, 83, 93, 99, 147, 191, 226, 283, 287; Scrapbook, W. W. Mills Collection, Archives, University of Texas Library.

72. Lucadia Niles (Mrs. E. M.) Pease, to Juliet Niles, April 18, 1875, in Graham-Pease Collection, Archives, Austin Public Library.

73. Following Hamilton's death his family was well provided for. Thanks to the genorosity of Morgan Hamilton, the widow and children benefited from a trust established in their behalf, consisting of a large amount in bonds and valuable properties in Austin. Morgan C. Hamilton's will, as cited; copy of the trust in hands of Frank Woodburn, grandson of A. J. Hamilton, who has given the author permission to use it; George E. Shelley, "The Semicolon Court of Texas," *South-Western Historical Quarterly*, XLVIII, pp. 449-468; A. J. Hamilton's Bible, in possession of John H. Chiles, great-grandson of A. J. Hamilton, who has allowed author to inspect it; Records of the Oakwood Cemetery, Austin.

manner of his passing had poignant overtones. It echoed, however faintly, the bewilderment and tribulation of the era just closed—a troubled era to which Andrew Jackson Hamilton, had brought a measure of rationality and relief.

By the spring of 1875 when Hamilton died, time had mellowed the hearts of many of his former political enemies. His sudden death cast a shadow over Austin. The people of the city turned out en masse to his funeral, demonstrating their respect for his memory. The funeral services were held in the Capitol, with several orators delivering eulogies. A guard of firemen, a military troop, and a large cortege of mourners accompanied the body to Oakwood Cemetery. The Supreme Court recessed for the day. A committee of prominent lawyers drafted a series of resolutions appropriate to the occasion. While admitting to differences with Hamilton at various times, members of the committee acknowledged and praised his character, integrity, patriotism, and genius.[74]

Evaluations of Hamilton as a historical figure have usually been made within the context of the Civil War and Reconstruction. Among those sympathetic to the Southern cause, he has remained a traitor or, at best, a scalawag. On the contrary, Unionists, especially in the North, have continued to regard him as a leader of exceptional courage, patriotism, and eloquence. This disagreement has persisted for a century.

An objective appraisal of Hamilton's career requires attention to aspects of it more fundamental than the mere colorful or controversial. Although on occasion he may have acted impulsively and spoken intemperately, Hamilton was in all essential respects a man of judgment and moderation. When endowed with power—as when he served as Provisional Governor and Associate Justice of the Military Supreme Court— he exercised power with commendable fairness and restraint. On several occasions, he rose to the level of true statesmanship. Texans will not forget his defiance and defeat of the Radical Republicans in the Reconstruction Convention of

1868-69 when they attempted to disfranchise the Conservative Democrats of the State, or his opposition to the corrupt railroad interests in the Twelfth Legislature, or his courageous and successful fight against E. J. Davis and the tyrannies of the Davis regime.

On the broader scene—that of the nation—Hamilton deserves even greater recognition. Without doubt, he will be remembered most for his stand in behalf of the Constitution and the Union. Pledging himself to this cause early in his career, he never waivered in supporting it. In this light, he should be honored for the efforts he made, the risks he took, and the calumnies he bore in pursuing the dominant purpose of his life—the defense of the American nation during the greatest crisis of its history.

74. Austin *Evening News,* June 8, 1875.

INDEX

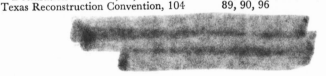

The text of this book is set in a type designed by John Baskerville in 1757 in England—the first to increase the contrast in thick and thin strokes and to sharpen the serifs. The titles are in Century roman with italics. The printing is by the Hill Printing Company, the binding by El Paso Bookbindery, the design and production plans by Carl Hertzog—all of El Paso, Texas.